THE INDEPENDENT GUIDE TO TOKYO DISNEY RESORT 2020

G. COSTA

Limit of Liability and Disclaimer of Warranty:
The publisher has used its best efforts in preparing this book, and the information provided herein is provided "as is." Independent Guides and the author make no representation or warranties concerning the accuracy or completeness of the contents of this book and expressly disclaims any implied warranties of merchantability or fitness for any particular purpose and shall in no event be liable for any loss of profit or any other damage, including but not limited to special, incidental, consequential, or other damages.

Please read all signs before entering attractions, as well as the terms and conditions of any companies used. Prices are approximate and do fluctuate.

Copyright Notice:
Contents copyright © 2012-2020 Independent Guides. All rights reserved. No part of this document or the related files may be reproduced or transmitted in any form, by any means (electronic, photocopying, recording, or otherwise) without the prior written permission of the publisher, unless it is for personal use. Some images and text are copyright © The Walt Disney Company or The Oriental Lanmicrd Company and affiliates and subsidiaries. This guide is not a The Walt Disney Company product, not is it endorsed by said company, or any other companies featured herein.

Contents

Introduction

Tokyo Disneyland Resort is an incredible place where dreams come true every day.

On 15th April 1983, Tokyo Disneyland opened – at the time, it was one park and the first venture for Disney outside of the USA. Disney had to be careful to balance the Asian culture with the American values that the company was founded upon. Tokyo Disneyland incorporates the best of the American Magic Kingdom Park and Disneyland Park, with new concepts unique to this location.

The Tokyo Disney Resort is not actually located in the city of Tokyo due to the vast amount of land needed. It is in Urayasu, Chiba Prefecture, which is to the east of the city. It is a 15-minute train ride from the city center.

The resort has flourished ever since 1983, and less than 20 years later, in 2001, a second theme park – Tokyo DisneySea – opened. DisneySea was a unique park, unlike anything seen anywhere around the world, with an incredibly high level of theming and many unique attractions. Many still say that DisneySea remains the best theme park in the world.

Today the resort comprises two theme parks, a shopping complex, nine on-site hotels (of which four are operated by Disney), and

even a private monorail system.

The Tokyo Disney Resort is not owned or operated by The Walt Disney Company, but by an enterprise called The Oriental Land Company. It is a unique relationship whereby Disney designs everything that gets built, but the resort is owned and run by another company under a license. The partnership works fantastically, and Tokyo Disneyland is often referred to as the "gold standard" for Disney resorts.

Guests who have visited other Disney theme park resorts will no doubt recognize many elements of the parks, and there is a certain feeling of familiarity. Still, there is so much that is unique to the resort to make it worth a visit.

Park guests may also be surprised by how busy the resort feels in Tokyo – there are always a lot of people here. Tokyo Disneyland was

the third most visited theme park in the world within 17.9 million visitors in 2018, and Tokyo DisneySea was the fourth most visited with 14.7 million visitors. The Greater Tokyo Region is also home to over 38 million inhabitants, so it is easy to see how the parks can be this busy.

This sizeable local population leads to crowding as many park guests own annual passes, so they can visit as often as they like. Regulars will happily wait 3 or 4 hours for their favorite ride as they can come back another day and do the other rides. There isn't really an "off-season" at this theme park resort. Foreign visitors are very much in the minority at the resort.

Now that you have some background on the resort, it is time to start planning your trip!

Planning a trip to the Tokyo Disney Resort can be daunting. You have to think about transport, accommodation, food, park tickets, spending money, etc. This section aims to get you prepared by following the steps below. All of these steps are further developed in the chapters that follow in this guide. .

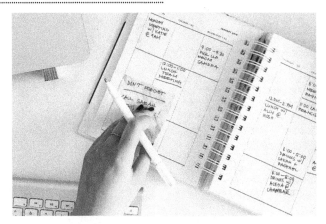

• **Decide how you want to get to the resort** – will you be flying in, driving, or taking a train? If you are using public transport, be sure to check what time you will arrive at the resort and when you will be leaving so that you can plan your days accordingly.

• **Decide whether you want to stay on-site or off-site.** Do you want the convenience of being near the magic? Or, do you want to stay elsewhere?

• **Study the theme park maps** at the back of this guide and the official park maps at bit.ly/tdrmaps. Combine the maps with the details in this book and decide which attractions and shows you want to visit. Circle the ones you want to visit on your map or write them down. Knowing roughly where the park attractions are is essential to making the most of your visit. You do not have to memorize the map, but looking at it in advance will save you valuable time once you arrive.

• **Park opening hours vary wildly**, the parks can open as early as 8:00 am and close as late as 1:00 am on certain days of the year. The latest hours are on Tokyo Disney Resort's website at bit.ly/tdrcalendar. Here you

can see the park hours for the next six months. Also, you can click on any date for a Times Guide that tells you when the parades and shows are taking place and the locations and times the characters are set to appear – this is very useful to know in advance.

• As **Tokyo Disney Resort is open 365 days a year**, it does not set aside a time of the year to close and perform its maintenance as most other theme parks do. Instead, the resort temporarily closes rides, shows, attractions, and park areas for refurbishment throughout the year. This is done once a year per attraction, usually during periods of lower attendance to limit the impact on guests. Refurbishments are

published with up to six months' notice. If there is a particular attraction you want to experience, make sure to check out the refurbishment schedule at bit.ly/tdrschedule.

• **If you are traveling from outside Japan**, be sure to bring plug adapters (and possibly power converters), as sockets in Japan may differ from your home country.

• **Make sure you get your Japanese Yen in advance.** Do not rely on buying currency at the airport. We recommend getting a pre-paid currency card that you can top up or using a credit or debit card with a 0% currency conversion rate. It is always handy to have some yen in cash.

Japan: Know Before You Go

Visiting Japan and the Tokyo Disney Resort is an exciting experience, yet it can be a daunting prospect for many – particularly Westerners who may never have step foot in Asia before. This section aims to help dispel some of the worries that you have about your visit.

Visa

Important: Please take this Visa section with a pinch of salt – regulations and rules are always changing, so be sure to check that this information is still current before you book your trip. Planning is key!

As of September 2019, 68 different countries have Visa Exemption Arrangements with Japan. This means that nationals of these countries can enter Japan without needing a visa. For most of these countries, visitors may stay for a period of up to 90 days. At the time of writing, these countries are: Andorra, Argentina, Australia, Austria, Bahamas, Barbados, Belgium, Bulgaria, Canada, Chile, Costa Rica, Croatia, Cyprus, Czech Republic, Denmark, Dominican Republic, El Salvador, Estonia, Finland, Former Yugoslav Republic of Macedonia, France, Germany, Greece, Guatemala, Honduras, Hong Kong, Hungary, Iceland, Ireland, Israel, Italy, Latvia, Lesotho, Liechtenstein, Lithuania, Luxembourg, Macao, Malaysia, Malta, Mauritius, Mexico, Monaco, Netherlands, New Zealand, Norway, Poland, Portugal, Republic of Korea, Romania, San Marino, Serbia, Singapore, Slovakia,

Slovenia, Spain, Surinam, Sweden, Switzerland, Taiwan, Tunisia, Turkey, United Kingdom, United States, and Uruguay.

Visitors from the United Arab Emirates have a Visa-Free period of stay of 30 days.

Visitors from the following three countries may only stay up to 15 days – this should still be plenty of time for a visit to Tokyo Disney Resort and the area and city around it: Indonesia, Thailand, and Brunei.

Please note you may need an electronic passport (with a chip in it and Machine Readable) for visa exemption to apply to your country. Most countries have now issued machine Readable passports for many years.

Even if you are the subject of a visa exemption arrangement, permission to enter Japan remains at the discretion of the immigration authorities. We advise that you should take supporting documents with you for immigration inspection at the airport, such as a return flight ticket, details of your trip and accommodation, and evidence of sufficient funds for your stay.

Residents from countries not listed above will need to go through the process of obtaining a visa for their visit. These include China, Russia, the Philippines, and Vietnam, amongst many others.

A guide from the official national tourism organization can be found at bit.ly/japanvisainfo.

Payments, Tipping and Currency

Japan uses the Japanese Yen as its unit of currency. At the time of writing, ¥1000 JPN is approximately $9.15 US, £6.86 GBP, or €8.22 EUR.

Japan is still primarily a cash-based society and has been slow to adopt internet banking and 24/7 ATMs. Many visitors are caught out by ATMs that only open from 9:00 am to 5:00 pm, or shops that don't accept credit cards. The situation is improving, but for the time being, get used to carrying cash. You can relax —

Tokyo's incredibly low crime rates make carrying cash a safe option.

The Tokyo Disney Resort does accept both cash and credit/debit cards at all Table Service and Counter Service restaurants, as well as shops. Most locations swipe cards without the need for a PIN, and you must have a signature on the back of your card.

An important note is that if you are paying by cash at a shop or restaurant, it is customary not to hand the money to the cashier, but instead, you place it in a tray or pot. Your change may be returned to you in the tray as well or directly to your hand.

Please note that there is no tipping in Japan, and if you attempt to tip, it will likely be refused – the Japanese don't understand why you would pay extra for a service you have already paid for. Most Japanese would also consider it rude and confusing to receive a gratuity, so please don't do it.

The Japanese People

For hundreds of years, Japan was closed off from the rest of the world, so it is no surprise to hear that Japan is incredibly homogenous, even today. Only 2.2% percent of Japan's population is non-Japanese, with 0.6% Chinese, 0.4% Korean, and 0.3% Vietnamese being the three largest foreign populations. The reason for this is Japan's strict immigration policies.

Although it is tough to become a resident of Japan, the Japanese are very welcoming to visitors, often going to great lengths to help tourists. Tokyo has the highest population of English speakers in the country, but even when residents don't have much English ability, they will do their best to help you. Don't be afraid to ask for directions from passersby or for help in a shop, but also

do not expect most people to speak English. In most locations, there will be at least one or two members of staff who do speak a reasonable level of English – in more touristy areas, English will not be a problem.

Visitors may also be overwhelmed by the level of politeness they receive in Japan! In our opinion, no customer service anywhere else rivals Japan's!

Shops, particularly department stores, and restaurant staff obey strict rules of politeness, adopting keigo, a highly stylized polite form of Japanese, to greet customers and conduct business.

If you don't understand what's going on, request 'easy Japanese' or simply smile—staff will not be offended if you don't understand.

The Language Barrier

Although English education is a big part of Japan's school curriculum, many shy Japanese people struggle to master English. Once you leave the tourist destinations and start exploring Tokyo, people are less confident in their English-speaking ability. If you step into a shop and the assistant immediately disappears, don't be offended! They've probably gone to find someone with better English skills to assist you.

Visitors to Tokyo Disney Resort do have it a bit easier than in other parts of Japan

– all signs and food menus have both Japanese and English language translations. Many shows have a mix of Japanese and English – songs are usually in English with the show script in Japanese. The stories are generally easy enough to follow, even without understanding the language – a few shows also have handheld subtitling units available.

In our experience, the majority of the Cast Members speak very little (or no) English, but they will try to help where possible.

At the hotels, and Guest Relations in the theme parks, you will find at least one member of staff who will speak fluent English. A translation app can come in excellent use!

The Tokyo Metro, Rail, and Bus systems are well signposted in English, with next stop announcements made in both Japanese and English.

As you would expect, if you visit remote locations in Japan, English is likely not to be spoken at all.

Food

Westerners visiting Tokyo, Tokyo Disney Resort, and Japan, in general, should be aware that the food they will encounter will be very different from that which they are used to back home.

Be sure to try some of the local delicacies when in Japan – at the Disney Resort, you will find an abundance of Western food,

but this is not necessarily the case throughout the rest of Japan.

By the entrance of many restaurants, both at Disney and throughout Japan, you may find a stand with plastic depictions of food items to help you visualize what the food looks like.

Mobile Phones, Internet Access and Wi-Fi

Avoid roaming networks in Japan due to the often-exorbitant cost of this service. Also, mobile phone networks in Japan are not necessarily compatible with smartphones from other countries (this is not usually an issue with Apple and Android devices), and non-Japanese residents are not usually able to buy a SIM card as they can do in many

other countries.

The solution is Docomo, a SIM card that you can pre-order before arrival in Japan. It can be shipped to specific locations in Japan, such as airports or tourist information centers. This SIM card will allow you to use data while in Japan, but you will not be able to make or receive phone calls or

text messages – the coverage is excellent. Pricing is about ¥2,500, including tax and delivery for an unlimited data card valid for eight days. Many other services are available.

We recommend looking at Klook and comparing which option works best for you. This website is an excellent one-stop-shop for entertainment and tickets in Japan and Asia. The Docomo sim card can be purchased at bit.ly/japansimcards.

You can get an exclusive ¥350-450 discount on your first booking by signing up at this special link - http://bit.ly/klookinvite There are also Wi-Fi hotspot

rental services such as Uroaming at the airports. You can book this at Klook at bit.ly/klookjapwifi from ¥126 per day per device, or ¥281 for unlimited data.

Wi-Fi access is not available at the Tokyo Disney Resort theme parks. The Disney hotels do have free Wi-Fi access, however. Free public Wi-Fi is not common

throughout Japan – Starbucks is a good bet if you see one. Over 200 Metro and Toei Subway stations also have free Wi-Fi.

We highly recommend having data access in Japan for translation purposes, navigation purposes, and seeing the wait times for rides and show schedules at the theme parks.

Weather and Travel Patterns

Tokyo's weather varies dramatically between seasons. The best times to visit are during Spring and Fall when mellow weather makes for comfortable traveling and produces beautiful scenery.

Spring
Spring temperatures range from 6°C to 22°C (43°F to 72°F) during the day. There is a second short rainy season in Spring, but apart from occasional showers, the weather is generally reasonable. Beware of traveling in early May. Golden Week, a string of national holidays at the end of April and start of May, is an incredibly popular time for Japanese people to travel.

Summer
Summer is time for the Obon festival, where families travel home to tend to their ancestral graves. It is also the time for fireworks and summer festivals. Beer

gardens spring up, offering relaxed evening dining under the open sky. It is also uncomfortably humid, particularly during the rainy season in June and July.

Invest in a good umbrella as raincoats are uncomfortable in Tokyo's summer heat. Summer temperatures range from 19°C to 32°C (66°F to 90°F) during the day, but the humidity means that the actual temperature feels much higher. Make sure to stay hydrated and keep cool.

Fall/Autumn
Autumn is when the bulk of Japan's school holidays take place, so family-orientated attractions (such as the Tokyo Disney Resort) are extremely crowded during this time.

Tokyo sees a rainy season in the Fall/Autumn, as frequent typhoons lash the capital with heavy rain and wind. The days following a typhoon are incredibly calm

and fine, perfect exploring weather. Autumn temperatures range from 9°C to 27°C (48°F to 81°F during the day.

Winter
Snow in Tokyo is relatively rare, and the weather tends to be crisp rather than chilly. The New Year period is especially busy as businesses end the year with bonnenkai, a lavish party. Japanese people celebrate Christmas with friends or dates (if they celebrate it at all) and travel home to spend the New Year period with their family.

Like Obon and Golden Week, New Year is a peak travel time in Japan. This a fun time to visit Tokyo, but be careful to make your travel arrangements well in advance to ensure that you don't end up stranded. Daytime temperatures range from 2°C to 12°C (35°F to 54°F).

Weather Averages by Month - First in Celcius, then in Fahrenheit in brackets

January	2-8 (36-46)	May	14-21 (57-70)	September	20-26 (68-79)
February	2-9 (36-48)	June	18-24 (64-75)	October	15-20 (59-68)
March	5-12 (41-54)	July	22-28 (72-82)	November	9-15 (48-59)
April	10-17 (50-63)	August	23-29 (73-84)	December	4-11 (39-52)

Getting to Tokyo Disney Resort

By far, the most convenient way for international visitors to arrive in Tokyo (and access Tokyo Disney Resort) is by plane.

Tokyo is connected to the world by its two International Airports. Upon arrival in Japan, visitors must endure a strict immigration process that includes a fingerprint check and photo; this often leads to long queues at immigration. To be sure that you do not miss connecting trains, allow yourself an hour or more here. Once through, if you are traveling extensively across Japan and plan on collecting the Japan Rail Pass, allow yourself even more time.

Narita Airport

Narita Airport is the older of Tokyo's two airports and handles most international flights. It is 58 km from Tokyo Disney Resort. It has recently added a third terminal to accommodate budget airlines within Japan. Terminals One and Two are connected to Tokyo by a variety of train and bus options that take travelers directly to transport hubs Tokyo, Nippori, Ueno, and Shinagawa. To get to Terminal Three, you must first reach Terminal Two and transfer via the 3-minute courtesy shuttle bus, or a 15-minute walk along the connecting pathway.

Bus: Limousine Bus
The Limousine Bus is the most convenient way to travel, taking you directly from the airport to Tokyo Disney Resort, including both theme parks. Some buses also drop-off at Tokyo Disney's hotels. Limousine isn't a reference to the car, but a brand of coaches that pride themselves on their quality and comfort. Unlike most Japanese buses, you purchase the ticket before getting on the bus from the Narita Airport Limousine Bus Ticket Counter. You cannot pre-purchase tickets online. The Limousine bus makes stops at Terminals 1, 2, and 3.

A one-way ticket from Narita to Tokyo Disney Resort is ¥1,900 for adults and ¥950 for children. The bus trip from the airport to Tokyo Disney Resort takes about 1 hour, and these journey times are usually pretty reliable. However, if you choose to take the bus, make sure you leave yourself plenty of time when returning to the airport in case of delays. The buses depart Narita Terminal 3 for Tokyo Disney Resort from 08:00 to 18:00.

When returning from Tokyo Disneyland (bus stop 3) to the airport, with buses running from 07:25 to 19:30. The journey is 1 hour from Tokyo Disneyland and 90 minutes from Tokyo DisneySea due to the extra stops at hotels. For bus schedules, see limousinebus.co.jp/en/infor mation/.

If you arrive after 18:00, you may want to get the Limousine Bus service to Shin-Urayasu Station instead (2.5 miles from the

resort). From here, you can get the train (Keiyo Line) or a quick 10-minute taxi ride. The last bus bound for Shin-Urayasu station leaves the airport at 20:30, so this buys you an extra bit of time.

If you have the option of taking the Limousine bus, it is the fastest, most comfortable, and most affordable option to get to the resort from the airport.

Rail: Naria Skyaccess + JR Keiyo/Musashino
This option only involves two trains to get to the resort and is much cheaper than the two following options, so it should be your preferred route if you are using rail between the airport and Tokyo Disney Resort.

Catch the Narita Skyaccess at Narita Airport. Ride the Skyaccess for about 30 minutes to Higashi-Matsudo Station. Here, buy a JR ticket to Maihama station. The total price should be ¥1,270, with a journey time of 1 hour 10 minutes. Allow 1 hour 30 minutes with luggage and to buy your tickets.

Rail: Skyliner + JR Yamanote + JR Keiyo/Musashino

This option involves using three trains to reach the resort. Firstly, board the Skyliner at Narita Airport. Ride the Skyliner for approximately 40 minutes (cost: ¥2,520) to Nippori Station – this is a non-stop trip, and trains run at 40-minute intervals. At Nippori Station, you will need to buy a JR ticket to Maihama.

Take the JR Yamanote Line to Tokyo Station (about 10 minutes), then inside the same station transfer to either the JR Keio Line or JR Musashino Line and get off at Maihama (15 minutes) – this is Tokyo Disney Resort's station. In total, this journey will take you about 1 hour 20 minutes, plus the time to buy both tickets and the pain of moving around with luggage, so allow 2 hours realistically. The total cost of this trip is ¥2,910.

Rail: Narita Express (N'EX) + JR Keiyo/Musashino

This option only involves two trains to get to the resort. Catch the JR Narita Express to Tokyo station; this will take 1 hour, and trains run at 30-minute intervals. At Tokyo Station, you will need to buy an extension ticket to Maihama Station (15 minutes) – this is Tokyo Disney Resort's station. This option takes just as long as the above rail option but requires one less change. The total cost of this trip is ¥2,900.

To decide between the three above rail options, use Google Maps, which shows you the options in real-time.

Taxi

Tokyo has numerous taxi companies at the airport. Ahead of the Olympic Games, some companies offer interpretation services in several languages, including English, but do not expect all taxi drivers to speak the language.

A taxi may be convenient, but it isn't cheap. Depending on traffic congestion, the ride from Tokyo Disney Resort to the airport takes about 1 hour and usually costs ¥20,000 to ¥35,000. Some taxis require passengers to pay the highway tolls to the airport, increasing the fare. Ask for an estimate of the price before getting in.

Narita Airport Shuttles

The airport is served by several airport shuttle companies, including Tokyo Limo, Super Shuttle, Blacklane, TT Shuttle, and GO Airport Shuttle. All can be booked in advance through a website such as www.airportshuttles.com. Fares range from ¥33,615 for a 3-seater vehicle to ¥103,566 for an ultimate luxury experience. A taxi makes more sense than this, to be perfectly honest.

Rental Car

There are various rental car options available at Narita Airport, but driving in Tokyo is not recommended. In addition to the difficulties of navigating Tokyo's busy streets, parking in the capital is an issue. Drivers in Japan are legally required to provide proof of a parking space for their vehicle, so there are not a lot of free parking options, and parking laws are strictly enforced. Overnight street parking is also illegal.

As you can imagine, this means that Tokyo Disney Resort takes advantage of this and charges for each night's parking at a rate of ¥1,000 to ¥2,000 at the hotels. Theme park parking is ¥2,500 to ¥3,000 per day, and cars may not be left overnight.

While many hotels and attractions have parking spaces available for guests, most locals use public transport, so the number of parking spaces is limited. Request a parking space when you make your hotel bookings or you may find yourself out of luck.

If you wish to rent a vehicle, car rental agencies have desks at the airport. To drive in Japan, you must obtain an International Drivers Permit in your home country. Travelers from some countries must get a translation of their driving license to drive in Japan.

Finally, the Japanese drive on the left side of the road, unlike most of the world.

Haneda Airport

Tokyo International Airport - or Haneda, as it is commonly known - is one of the busiest airports in Asia. The majority of flights are domestic, but increasing numbers of international flights are routed into Haneda. The airport is closer to the Tokyo Disney Resort than Narita Airport, only 21 km from Tokyo Station and only 23 km from Tokyo Disney Resort. Haneda is well served by a variety of public transport options.

Haneda consists of three terminals. The international terminal is connected to the two domestic terminals by a free shuttle bus, and from there, the numerous transport options. However, passengers arriving between midnight and 05:00 will find themselves looking at either a steep taxi fare or long wait as the public transport does not run during this period.

Bus: Limousine Bus

You can board a direct Limousine bus from the airport to Tokyo Disney Resort. This is the easiest, the fastest and most hassle-free option provided the timetable works with your scheduled flight arrival time. The journey takes 25-40 minutes and can be boarded from Haneda Airport Terminal 1 or 2 (there is also an irregular service from the International Terminal). Allow additional time for hotel drop-off.

The first bus leaves the airport at 07:35, and buses run every 10-20 minutes. The last bus leaves at 19:00. Buses leave Tokyo Disneyland to return to the airport between 7:30 and 19:00 every 10-20 minutes.

A one-way adult ticket is ¥850. The child fare is ¥430.

Rail: Monorail + Rinkai Line + JR Keiyo Line

The monorail takes you directly to and from Haneda's International Terminal in style. It takes only 14 minutes to travel from the International Terminal to Tennozu Isle Station Monorail station (which links up to JR and subway lines) and, making for fast and convenient transfers. The monorail runs every three to five minutes, from approximately 5:15 am to midnight. You can take two items of luggage with a combined weight of 30 kg onto the monorail.

You will need to take the monorail from Haneda Airport to Tennozu Isle Station. Here, you change to the Rinkai Line to Shin-Kiba Station (a 10-minute ride), followed by a short hop from Shin-Kiba Station to Maihama Station on the JR Keiyo Line. The total fare is ¥920 one-way; the journey takes about 50 minutes.

Rail: Keikyu Airport Line + Hibiya Line + JR Keiyo Line

This is an alternative route. Ride the Keiyu Airport Line to Higashi-ginza Station for about 25 minutes. Here, transfer to the Hibiya Line for about 4 minutes to Hatchobori Station. Finally, here transfer again to the JR Keiyo Line for a 14-minute ride to Maihama Station. The total fare is ¥800 one-way, and the journey takes about 55 minutes in total.

Taxi

Taxis run 24 hours to and from Haneda Airport, making them a convenient option when the trains and buses are not running. Taxis are the most expensive option, with a one-way trip from the airport to Tokyo Disney Resort costing ¥7,000 to ¥11,000, depending on traffic conditions. The journey takes about 30 minutes.

Rental Car

Like Narita Airport, Japan's major rental car agencies have desks at Haneda Airport, but travel by car in Tokyo is not recommended. If you need a car, rental car desks are located at all Haneda's terminals.

Tokyo Disney Resort from Tokyo

Tokyo is a vast city, and therefore, we are not able to list the ways to reach the Tokyo Disney Resort from everywhere around the city. Instead, here we list several routes from areas popular with tourists.

If you are arriving from another Japanese city on the Shinkansen ("bullet trains"), you will come into Tokyo Station – follow the directions to Disney from the appropriate section below.

Shibuya

For the fewest transfers, ride the JR Saikyo Line from Shibuya station to Shin-Kiba Station. Here, transfer for the Keiyo Line to Maihama Station. The total fare is ¥720 and the journey should take about 35 minutes.

The same journey in a taxi will take 25 to 50 minutes, and cost ¥7,000 to ¥12,000.

Shinjuku

The simplest route for this rail journey is to take the same as the above. Take the JR Saikyo Line from Shibuya station to Shin-Kiba Station. Here, transfer for the Keiyo Line to Maihama Station. The total fare is ¥730, and the journey should take about 40 minutes.

The same journey in a taxi will take 30 minutes to 1 hour, and cost ¥8,000 to ¥12,500.

Ginza / Tokyo Station area

This is a straightforward trip on the Keiyo Line from Tokyo Station to Maihama Station, which should take 13 to 17 minutes. The fare is ¥220.

The same journey in a taxi will take 15 minutes to 40 minutes and cost ¥5,000 to ¥9,000.

Asakusa

For your rail journey, ride the Asakusa Line from Asakusa Station to Ningyocho Station (about 7 minutes). Here transfer to the Hibiya Line to Hatchobori Station (about 3 minutes). Finally, ride the Keiyo Line from Hatchobori Station to Maiahama Station (about 15 minutes). In total, with transfers, this ride should take about 35 minutes. The fare is ¥500.

The same journey in a taxi will take 25 minutes to 40 minutes and cost ¥6,000 to ¥10,500.

Hotels
Booking Your Hotel

We recommend booking your Tokyo Disney Resort hotel through the official online reservation system - https://reserve.tokyodisneyresort.jp/en/hotel/list/.

Reservations made for Deluxe hotels will require a ¥30,000 reservation deposit per stay, with the remainder payable on checkout. For Value hotels, this is a ¥15,000 deposit.

Reservations open day by day at 11:00 am Japan Time 5 months in advance. All the official Disney hotels sell out and you WILL need to book on the day that reservations open for a chance at getting a room, particularly if you want a Harbor-view room at the Hotel MiraCosta (for these you will need to book at exactly 11:00 am Japan Time five months in advance). After this, room availability is more limited and will sell out at peak times very quickly.

For third-party hotels, you

may prefer to use another hotel booking engine such as Hotels.com, for example. You can also book all Disney hotels (except the Hotel Miracosta) on third party websites, too, subject to availability.

Pricing in this section is only meant as a comparative example and will fluctuate based on dates and availability. Pricing is based on two adults in one room.

In this section, we cover both Disney-run hotels and 'Official Hotels' as these are the ones you will want to stay in near the theme parks. There are also two further categories of hotels, including Partner Hotels (Hotel Emion Tokyo Bay, Mitsui Garden Hotel Prana Tokyo Bay, Urayasu Brighton Hotel Tokyo Bay, Oriental Hotel Tokyo Bay), and a vast selection of Good Neighbor Hotels. The differences between all these styles of hotels can be seen in the table that follows.

Hotel Benefit Spotlight: Pre-Check-In

This service allows you to do all the check-in formalities before the official check-in time of 3:00 pm. You will receive your room key in advance, and your baggage will be delivered to your room so that you can head straight to your room when you return later in the day. The only strange caveat is that your room will only be ready from 4:30 pm, and not the usual 3:00 pm time.

The pre-check-in service is available either at your Disney deluxe hotel from 7:00 am to 1:00 pm, and at the Tokyo Disney Resort Welcome Center located by JR Maihama Station from 7:30 am to 4:00 pm.

Hotel Categories

The Tokyo Disney Resort has several categories of hotel available - here we list them all, and their benefits.

	Disney Hotel - Deluxe	Disney Hotel - Value	Resort Official Hotels	Resort Partner Hotels	Resort Good Neighbor Hotels
Transport to the Theme Parks	Walking, Shuttle Bus and Monorail	Shuttle Bus (15-20 minutes)	Disney Cruiser Shuttle Bus	Shuttle Bus run by Hotels (no reservations, scheduled)	Shuttle Bus run by Hotels (reservations required)
15 Minutes Early Theme Park Entry (Happy 15)	Yes	Yes	No	No	No
Disney Touches	Disney-designed, sale of special park tickets, Disney shop, and exclusive merchandise	Disney-designed, sale of special park tickets, Disney shop, and exclusive merchandise	Disney shop	Disney shop	None
Baggage Delivery Service	Included - from TDR Welcome Center	Extra charge – ¥400 per bag – from Bon Voyage	Included - from TDR Welcome Center	Extra charge – ¥400 per bag – from Bon Voyage	Not available
Guaranteed Park Entry	Yes	Yes	Yes	No	No

The Tokyo Disney Resort Welcome Center

The Welcome Center, located next to JR Maihama Station, provides support for Hotel services at the resort to ensure a convenient and pleasant stay. It is ideally located for guests arriving at the resort by train.

The Welcome Center is split into two levels. On the first floor (downstairs), services here are for Tokyo Disney Resort Official Hotels. The second floor of the Welcome Center is reserved for deluxe Disney Hotel guests. For clarity, this is for guests staying at Disney Ambassador Hotel, Tokyo DisneySea Hotel MiraCosta, and Tokyo Disneyland Hotel.

What can I do at the Welcome Center?

You can use the Pre-check-in service, Baggage delivery to the hotel (no valuables, breakable items and beverages), buy your theme park tickets, and Disney Resort Line ticket pickup (only for Guests of Hotel MiraCosta and Tokyo Disneyland Hotel).

The Welcome Center is open from 7:30am to 5:00pm for deluxe Disney Hotel guests, and 8:00am to 3:00pm for Tokyo Disney Resort Official Hotels guests.

By visiting the Welcome Center upon arrival, you can have a smooth Tokyo Disney Resort experience and maximize your time. You can check-in for your hotel and go and enjoy the parks immediately while your luggage is transferred to your hotel with the Baggage Delivery Service.

You can also use the Welcome Center to pick up luggage sent from the Disney hotels and Tokyo Disney Resort Official Hotels (for an extra fee); this is the Station Delivery Service.

Vacation Packages

As well as booking your hotel using the Tokyo Disney Resort website, it is also possible to book a Vacation Package, which includes your accommodation, park tickets, Fastpasses, show reservations, and other goodies.

This is a great way to book everything in one go and get exclusive benefits. Vacation Package reservations open 6 months in advance to the day at 11:00 am Japan time. However, this is only suitable for guests wanting to do a 1-night or 2-night stay. In addition, Vacation Packages are significantly more expensive than booking items separately.

A Vacation Package includes:
- 2-Day Passport Special / 3-Day Magic Passport Special, which allows you to park-hop from the first day, unlike regular park tickets, which only let you park-hop from day 3
- Fastpasses valid on all attractions which offer this service. This can be a big time-saver and significantly ease your stay. With each package, you will receive a certain number of tickets for all Fastpass attractions (except the headliner rides), and a separate number of tickets for the big headliner rides (Beauty and the Beast, Toy Story Mania and Tower of Terror)
- Disney Resort Line Day Pass, to get between the parks easily
- Your accommodation with a choice of their Disney Hotels, Tokyo Disney Resort Official Hotels, or even Tokyo

Disney Resort Partner Hotels
- Free gift, e.g., tote bag, plush or toy game
- Free drinks throughout your stay per person
- Free original popcorn bucket (with one free popcorn serving) per room

For the ultimate Disney experience, this is a fantastic option.

Price comparison:
For a price comparison, we chose a 2-night stay in March 2020 for two adults at Tokyo DisneySea Hotel MiraCosta in a Tuscany Side Capitano Mickey Superior Room.

Booked via the Vacation Package website this 'Experience Attractions and Entertainment 3-Day Plan' included two reserved show tickets per person, and seven Fastpasses per person (one of these is valid on either Beauty and the Beast, Toy Story Mania and Tower of Terror), as well as all the other benefits. The price for this comes to ¥257,800 (approx. $2350 / £1800 / €2100) for the whole package, including two

mornings of breakfasts for two people.

Now, if we book this ourselves separately, the same hotel room comes to ¥118,800; a 3-Day Passport Special is ¥39,400, breakfast would be another ¥12,000. The total here is ¥170,200. The package is, therefore, ¥87,600 more expensive (approx. $800/£610/€715). That is a significant premium even if we value the gift, drinks and popcorn bucket at $100US, there is still a $700 premium for the package for 18 ride and show reservations; this is the equivalent of paying $40 per person for each ride and show reservation. The Fastpasses can be used at any time, however, which eliminates all the running around getting Fastpasses (although you can still do that!).

Therefore, if you are on a budget the package is probably not for you – if you want the simplicity of booking your whole trip in just a few minutes and are happy to pay a premium of about 50%, then this may be a good option for you.

Tokyo DisneySea Hotel MiraCosta

This 5-star, 502-room Deluxe hotel is Tokyo Disney Resort's flagship hotel. It is themed as an Italian fishing town and is the height of luxury. Enjoy staying 'inside' the Tokyo DisneySea theme park.

The Hotel MiraCosta is the most luxurious place to stay on-site, and is a genuinely opulent hotel. This hotel is located both inside and outside the DisneySea theme park, meaning that certain guest bedrooms and guest areas have views into the DisneySea theme park. This means you can wake up to the sight of Mount Prometheus, and go to sleep after watching Fantasmic from your bed.

There are three different sides to this hotel, each with a different ambiance and views: Tuscany, Venice, and Porto Paradiso. The Tuscany side is what guests see when entering the hotel and the theme park, guests staying here will not get views of the theme park. The Venice side of the hotel faces the hotel's Terme Venezia Spa & Pool area and the Palazzo Canals in Tokyo DisneySea Park. Finally, the Porto Paradiso side faces the Porto Paradiso area of the Mediterranean Harbor in Tokyo DisneySea Park.

The upgraded *Speciale* rooms and suites all include views of Tokyo DisneySea Park, and breakfast served at the private lounge called Salon dell'Amico.
Some *Speciale* rooms even have terraces overlooking the park (the Terrace Room starts at ¥110,500 per night).

The Hotel MiraCosta offers amenities such as a spa, an indoor pool and an outdoor pool. However, the use of these pools is not included in your stay and requires an extra fee. The spa offers a traditional onsen bath experience (no bathing attired allowed). The on-site gym closed in Spring 2019, and no alternative is offered. The outdoor pool is only open in the summer season. There is no coin-laundry or convenience/sundry store at this hotel. Note that guests with tattoos may be asked to cover these up in the pool and spa area.

There is a direct private entrance to Tokyo DisneySea theme park from within the hotel – this can only be used by hotel residents and those dining there. To reach Tokyo Disneyland Park, you take the direct walkway to the

monorail and ride it for about 5 minutes.

Check-in is at 3:00 pm, and check out is at noon. Guests of this hotel enjoy 15-minute's early entry into the theme parks with the Happy15 privilege.

As well as standard rooms (37m²), other room types include Triple Room (43 m²) – 3 beds, Porto Paradiso Side Harbor Room (60 m²) – 2 beds. Suites from 81m² to 199m² are also available.

The Harbor View rooms at this hotel sell out within minutes of being released – standard rooms, suites, and 'Speciale' concierge-level rooms are the most popular rooms at the entire Tokyo Disney Resort.

Breakfast: Not included.
Room prices:
- Tuscany Side Mickey

Superior Room (37 m²) – From ¥49,600 to ¥80,000.
- Venice Side Superior Room (37 m²) – From ¥49,600 to ¥80,000.
- Porto Paradiso Side Superior Room Piazza View (37 m²) – From ¥62,200 to ¥84,200.

- Porto Paradiso Side Superior Room Harbor View (37 m²) – From ¥62,200 to ¥84,200.
- Speciale Porto Paradiso Side Porto Paradiso Suite (81m²) – ¥185,000   .

Extras: Complimentary Wi-Fi, complimentary pass for

the Disney Resort Line monorail, private park entrance, spa and indoor swimming pool (year-round, extra charge), outdoor pool (summer only – additional charge), shipping counter – can send internationally.

Dining:

Oceano – Mediterranean cuisine. Serves breakfast (buffet), lunch and dinner (buffet or table service options). Breakfast: ¥3,200 for adults (ages 13+), ¥2,100 for juniors (ages 7-12), and ¥1,500 for children (ages 4-6). The Lunch buffet is priced at ¥4,200/¥3,000/¥2,000 respectively, and the dinner buffet is ¥5,800/¥3,600/¥2,600. There is a terrace where guests can step out and watch park shows on the harbor.
Silk Road Garden – Chinese cuisine. Table Service. Serves lunch and dinner. Lunch is priced from around ¥4,500 and dinner from ¥7,000.
BellaVista Lounge – Lobby lounge and Italian cuisine. Serves breakfast (buffet), lunch and dinner (table service). There is a view into the Mediterranean Harbor of Tokyo DisneySea park. Breakfast: ¥3,000 for adults (ages 13+), ¥1,900 for juniors (ages 7-12), and ¥1,300 for children (ages 4-6). Lunch is priced at ¥4,300/¥3,700/¥2,800 respectively, and the dinner buffet is ¥8,200/¥3,700/¥2,800.
Hippocampi – Poolside Bar. Serves soft drinks, sandwiches, snacks, and desserts from 10:00 am to 5:00 pm.

Tokyo Disneyland Hotel

The Tokyo Disneyland Hotel is a 5-star, 706-room Victorian-style Deluxe hotel located directly opposite Tokyo Disneyland Park.

From this hotel to the Tokyo Disneyland Park entrance is a 1-minute walk under the monorail station. To reach Tokyo DisneySea Park, you walk a few seconds to the monorail and ride it for about 7 minutes.

The hotel is a truly luxurious place to stay, and you will not be disappointed with a stay here. Conveniently, this hotel is also only a few minutes' walk from Maihama Station, making arriving at the resort very simple.

As well as standard rooms (37m²), other room types include the Alcove Room (40 m²) – up to 4 adults, Deluxe Room (48 m²) – up to 3 adults, Corner Room (59 m²) – up to 2 adults, Family Rooms (57m² to 93m²) – up to 5 adults with two separate bathrooms.

The hotel also features magical Disney character rooms themed to one of the following: Tinker Bell, Alice in Wonderland, Beauty and the Beast, and Cinderella. Each accommodates between 2 and 4 adults, with room sizes varying from 40m² to 71m². These rooms do not face the park, and instead, face the hotel's gardens and car entrance.

Concierge-level rooms all face Tokyo Disneyland Park, have access to the exclusive Marceline Salon, and have breakfast served in the Dreamers Lounge. These are available in all variety of sizes from the Superior Rooms (40 m²) to the Family Room (104 m²) with space for six adults. Finally, several suites are available, culminating in the vast Walt Disney Suite at 235m² in size.

Check-in is at 3:00 pm, and check out is at noon. Guests of this hotel enjoy 15-minute's early entry into the theme parks with the Happy15 privilege.

The hotel features three restaurants with a variety of cuisines. As well as a large Disney merchandise shop, the hotel also includes a handy mini-supermarket (Looking Glass Gifts), which the Hotel MiraCosta does not. This sells a huge range of food from bento boxes to sandwiches to sushi, potato chips, chocolate, as well as other necessities such as baby food and disposable diapers (but no medicine).

There is also an outdoor pool themed to Peter Pan, and an on-site coin laundry – the only on-site deluxe Disney hotel to have this. Guests with tattoos may be asked to cover these up in the pool area.

This hotel houses the Bibbidi Bobbidi Boutique in which little girls can be transformed into princesses in a full-service hair, make-up, and dress session. This is also available to guests not staying at the hotel. Prices vary from approximately ¥10,000 to ¥40,000, depending on which package is selected. An optional photo shoot is also available. Online booking of Bibbidi Bobbidi Boutique is only available in Japanese.

Breakfast: Not included.
Nightly Room Prices:
- Superior Room (37 m²) – From ¥39,000 to ¥65,900.
- Beauty and the Beast Character Room (61m²) – From ¥61,600 to ¥99,200.
- Standard Family Room (57 m²) – From ¥52,800 to ¥92,300.
- Concierge Superior Room (40m²) – From ¥64,200 to ¥102,600.
Extras: Complimentary Wi-Fi, complimentary pass for the Disney Resort Line

monorail, outdoor pool (summer only), laundry room, shipping counter – can send internationally.

Dining:

Sherwood Garden Restaurant – International cuisine. Buffet. Serves breakfast, lunch and dinner. Breakfast: ¥3,200 for adults (ages 13+), ¥2,100 for juniors (ages 7-12), and ¥1,500 for children (ages 4-6). Lunch is priced at ¥4,000/¥3,000/¥2,000 respectively, and dinner is ¥5,200/¥3,500/¥2,500.

Canna – Asian cuisine. Table Service. Serves lunch and dinner. This is a contemporary-style restaurant. From ¥3,000 for lunch and ¥6,000 for dinner.

Dreamers Lounge – Lobby lounge. Table Service. Serves breakfast (buffet), lunch and dinner. Offers great views out of large windows to Tokyo Disneyland Monorail Station and the park entrance, and a grand lobby atmosphere. Breakfast: ¥2,800 for adults (ages 13+), ¥1,700 for juniors (ages 7-12), and ¥1,000 for children (ages 4-6).

Disney Ambassador Hotel

This 504-room Deluxe Hotel is located next to Tokyo Disney Resort's dining and entertainment district, Ikspiari. The theme of this hotel is Hollywood-era Art Deco.

Despite being a deluxe-type hotel, this hotel does not have direct access to either theme park or a monorail station. However, Disney operates the free Disney Resort Cruiser shuttle buses to both theme parks, with a journey time of about five minutes. You can also walk to Tokyo Disneyland Park in about 15 minutes, and Tokyo DisneySea in 10 minutes. Hotel guests do not get free Disney Resort Line monorail passes.

This hotel features four dining locations, including one with character dining. There is also an outdoor pool (open in the summer only), a Disney shop, and a small convenience store selling food, snacks, baby food, diapers, and other necessities. There is no coin-laundry at this hotel.

The hotel also offers the free Chip'n Dale's Playground, open from 7:00 am to 8:00 pm daily for children aged 11 and under. This is not a daycare facility; children must be supervised.

Check-in is at 3:00 pm, and check out is at noon. Hotel guests enjoy 15-minutes early entry into one of the theme parks with the Happy15 privilege.

As well as standard rooms which sleep three adults (34m² to 38m²), other room types include the Superior Room (40 m²) – up to 3 adults, Triple Room (45 m²) – up to 3 adults, Palm Garden View (70 m²) – up to 2 adults, Junior Family Room (56 m²) – up to 4 adults, and Family Room (97 m²) – up to 5 adults.

The Ambassador Floor rooms and suites are the concierge-level with access to an exclusive lounge, and breakfast is included. Rooms range from the Mickey Mouse Room (38 m²) to Mickey's Penthouse Suite (150 m²).

As well as character rooms on the Ambassador Floor, the hotel features standard character rooms themed to the following: Donald Duck, Chip 'n Dale, and Stitch.

Breakfast: Not included.

Nightly Room Prices:
- Standard Floor Standard Room (34 m²) – From ¥30,000 to ¥67,500.
- Standard Floor Stitch Room (45 m²) – From ¥43,700 to ¥78,500.
- Ambassador Floor Mickey Mouse Room (41m² to 45m²) – From ¥50,900 to ¥97,800.
- Standard Floor Junior Family Room (56 m²) – From ¥54,400 to ¥87,400.
- Ambassador Floor Panorama Suite (97 m²) – From ¥94,500 to ¥149,000.

Extras: Complimentary Wi-Fi, Complimentary shuttle bus to the theme parks, outdoor pool (summer only), shipping counter – can send internationally.

Dining:

Chef Mickey – Character dining buffet with both Western and Japanese options. Serves breakfast, lunch and dinner. Breakfast is exclusively for guests staying at the Disney Ambassador Hotel. There is a 1 hour 30-minute limit to the buffet. Breakfast: ¥3,700 for adults (ages 13+), ¥2,400 for juniors (ages 7-12), and ¥1,700 for children (ages 4-6). Lunch and dinner are priced at ¥5,300/¥3,300/¥2,300, respectively.

Empire Grill – Californian cuisine with inspiration from Italy, Mexico, and Asia. Table Service. Serves lunch and dinner. There is a 2-hour time limit to meals here. Lunch starts from around ¥3,500 per person and dinner from ¥8,500.

Tick Tock Diner – Counter Service and Take-Out options from a 1950s-style diner with cakes, slices of bread, and sandwiches. This is the only counter service restaurant at any of the three deluxe Disney resorts. A sandwich meal is around ¥1,000.

Hyperion Lounge – Lobby Lounge. Serves a buffet breakfast, and table service lunch and dinner for drinks and snacks. There are no characters for meals here. Breakfast: ¥2,700 for adults (ages 13+), ¥1,700 for juniors (ages 7-12), and ¥1,000 for children (ages 4-6).

Tokyo Disney Celebration Hotel

This 702-room, 3.5-star Value hotel is the newest hotel at Tokyo Disney Resort, having opened in 2016. Unlike the three other Disney hotels covered earlier in this section, this hotel is not on-site at the resort, nor is it a luxury-style property. The hotel is split into two parts – Wish and Discover – and each has its own unique theming.

This value hotel is located about 6km (4 miles) away from the main resort in a different neighborhood. As this hotel has no access to the Disney Resort Line monorail, Disney offers complimentary Disney Resort Cruiser shuttle buses to both theme parks, with a journey time of about 20 minutes door-to-door.

For those wanting to stay at a Disney-branded hotel on a budget, this is a much more affordable option. The hotel also offers the benefit of early Happy15 admission and guaranteed park entry during crowded days.

However, in all honesty, we would recommend staying at one of the 'Official Hotels' on the Monorail Loop for a similar price for the convenience instead of having the 15-minute early entry. This hotel offers standard rooms for five adults too, which none of the other Disney hotels do.

The hotel features a Disney Fantasy merchandise shop and a sundry shop selling snacks and essentials such as diapers and baby food.

Check-in is at 3:00 pm, and check out is at 11:00 am. Guests of this hotel enjoy 15-minute's early entry into one of the theme parks with the Happy15 privilege. This hotel does not offer a pool.

As well as the Standard Rooms (29 m²) which sleep up to 4 adults, other room types include Triple Rooms (32 m²) – up to 3 adults, and Superior Rooms (35m² to 39m²) – up to 4 adults. There is also a Quintet Room (29 m²) with room to sleep five adults using a sofa daybed and bunk beds, in addition to two regular beds.

Breakfast: Not included.

Nightly Room Prices:
- Standard Room (29 m²) – From ¥17,600 to ¥49,000.
- Triple Room (32 m²) – From ¥19,800 to ¥50,400.
- Quintet Room (29 m²) – From ¥19,800 to ¥52,900.
- Superior Room (35m² to 38m²) – From ¥20,100 to ¥61,100.

Extras: Complimentary Wi-Fi, Complimentary shuttle bus service to the theme park.

Dining:

There is only one dining location in each of the two areas of the hotel; these are the Wish Café and Discover Café. Only a simple breakfast buffet is offered (6:00 am to 9:30 am), food is not available at this hotel after 9:30 am except for snacks from the sundry store. Breakfast is ¥1,500 for ages 12+, ¥500 for ages 4 to 11, and free for ages 3 and under.

Resort Official Hotels

The following six hotels are not Disney hotels and therefore do not enjoy pHappy15 entry, but they do offer guaranteed park entry. Although not operated by Disney, these are still Official Resort Hotels and are worth a look at. The Hilton and Sheraton, for example, may be useful to holders of hotel loyalty points or status.

Each of these hotels is located either directly by Bayside Station on the Disney Resort Line monorail or offers shuttle buses to this monorail station, offering convenient access to the theme parks. You will need to purchase tickets or passes to use the monorail directly at the station. Each of these hotels also offers a shuttle to JR Maihama station, which generally runs every 20 to 30 minutes on a set timetable.

Hotel Okura Tokyo Bay

This 427-room, 5-star hotel features spacious rooms (starting at 44m^2), and there are a variety of amenities, including an indoor swimming pool, a gym, a beauty salon, and a pharmacy.

The hotel is located directly next to Bayside Station on the Disney Resort Line monorail – you can either walk in 2 minutes or use the complimentary Disney Resort Cruiser shuttle to the monorail station. You can also walk directly to Tokyo Disneyland Park in 20 minutes, whereas Tokyo DisneySea is a lengthier 35-minute walk.

The hotel features several restaurants: Hagoromo serves Japanese-style dishes for breakfast, lunch, and dinner – it also serves Teppanyaki. Restaurant Fontana serves Western dishes for breakfast, lunch, and dinner. Tohkalin is a Chinese restaurant open for dinner (and lunch on select nights). Café Restaurant Terrace offers a buffet-style breakfast and dinner. There are also two bars on site.

Rooms offer complimentary Wi-Fi.

Nightly Room Prices: Rooms start at ¥15,000 to ¥33,000.

Hilton Tokyo Bay

This 4-star, 828-room hotel features both an indoor and (a seasonal) outdoor pool, an on-site gym, a children's playground, spa services, and more.

The hotel is located a 6-minute walk from Bayside Station on the Disney Resort Line monorail, or you can use the complimentary Disney Resort Cruiser shuttle to the monorail station. You can also walk directly to Tokyo Disneyland Park in 20 minutes, and Tokyo DisneySea in 40 minutes.

The hotel features several restaurants. Dynasty Restaurant serves Chinese food for lunch and dinner. Fresh Connection is a deli-style counter service location serving a wide variety of breakfast, lunch, dinner, and snack choices, including salads, pasta options, sandwiches, and pastries. Guests can order from their guest room or at the shop for pickup. Lounge O offers a dessert buffet in the afternoon. The Square: Accendo offers Mediterranean cuisine for lunch and dinner. The Square: Forest Garden offers a 25-meter-long buffet for breakfast, lunch, and dinner featuring dishes from around the world. Finally, The Square: Silva is a bar serving both alcoholic and non-alcoholic beverages, including coffee and cocktails.

Rooms do not offer complimentary Wi-Fi at this resort.

Nightly Room Prices: Rooms start at ¥18,000 to ¥39,000.

Sheraton Grande Tokyo Bay Hotel

This 1016-room, 4-star hotel features beautiful gardens, both an indoor and outdoor swimming pool, a gym, a spa, and a kid's playground.

The hotel is located next to Bayside Station on the Disney Resort Line monorail – you can either walk in 2 minutes or use the complimentary Disney Resort Cruiser shuttle to the station. You can also walk

directly to Tokyo Disneyland in 20 minutes, and Tokyo DisneySea in 35 minutes.

The hotel features several restaurants: Grand Café offers a buffet with Western and Asian options. Teppanyaki Restaurant Maihama offers Japanese cuisine. Galleria Café is a food court. Café Toastina is a casual grab-and-go location with coffee, cakes, a dessert

buffet, and a deli. Asuka is the resort's signature Japanese restaurant with multi-course dining and a sushi bar.

Rooms offer complimentary Wi-Fi. There is also a row of shops selling flowers and souvenirs, a drug store, and a barbershop.

Nightly Room Prices: Rooms start at ¥20,000 to ¥37,000.

Tokyo Bay Maihama Hotel First Resort

This 696-room, 4-star hotel features an outdoor pool and themed rooms.

This hotel is not located directly next to Bayside Station on the Disney Resort Line monorail. Instead, it is a 10-minute walk away, or you can use the complimentary

Disney Resort Cruiser shuttle to the monorail station. You can also walk directly to Tokyo Disneyland Park in 10 minutes, and Tokyo DisneySea in 35 minutes.

There are three restaurants at this hotel. California offers all-day buffet-style dining.

Hamakase is a Japanese-style restaurant. Finally, Sky Restaurant Carnival is on the top floor, and serves French cuisine.

Nightly Room Prices: Rooms start at ¥17,000 to ¥32,000 .

Tokyo Bay Maihama Hotel Club Resort

This 700-room, 4-star hotel features an impressive lobby and a waterside location. The hotel is more basic in terms of facilities than some other hotels in this section; although there are a small convenience store and beauty salon on-site, there is no gym or pool here.

This hotel is not directly next

to Bayside Station on the Disney Resort Line monorail. It is a 5-minute walk away, or you can use the complimentary Disney Resort Cruiser shuttle to the monorail station. You can also walk directly to Tokyo Disneyland Park in 20 minutes, and Tokyo DisneySea in 40 minutes.

There are four restaurants at this hotel. The Atrium serves food all day in a buffet style. Gyoan offers Japanese food in a Table Service set menu-style. Sur La Mer serves French-style food on the top floor. Finally, Patisserie is a coffee-shop style location.

Nightly Room Prices: Rooms start at ¥15,000 to ¥30,000.

Tokyo Bay Maihama Hotel

This 3-star, 428-room hotel is on the more basic side and offers a spa, but no pool.

This hotel is not directly next to Bayside Station on the Disney Resort Line monorail. It is a 7-minute walk away, or you can use the free Disney

Resort Cruiser shuttle to the monorail station. You can also walk directly to Tokyo Disneyland Park in 15 minutes, and Tokyo DisneySea in 40 minutes.

There are three dining locations. Restaurant Fine

Terrace is a Table Service restaurant with international cuisine. Café Brook is an all-day bar and coffee place. Hotel Bakery HoneyBee is an all-day bakery.

Nightly Room Prices: Rooms start at ¥17,000 to ¥37,000.

Tickets

There are many ways to buy park entry tickets for the Tokyo Disney Resort. Prices, special offers, and ticket lengths vary depending on where you buy your tickets. To help you choose the best option for you, here is a detailed look at TDR's ticket options.

Online Tickets and Tickets at the Park

Important: If you have booked a Vacation Package through the Tokyo Disney Resort website, you can skip this chapter, as your tickets are included in your package unless you specifically make a room-only reservation.

Guests who turn up at the Tokyo Disney Resort spontaneously can buy tickets at the booths at the entrance of each theme park. Guests can also purchase tickets in advance online – we would recommend doing this to save yourself time during your visit. Also, the theme parks do sell out of tickets on peak days, so there is the potential that if you wait to buy the tickets until the day of your visit, that you will not be able to get in.

Unlike many theme parks, the price of buying a ticket on the day and in advance is the same. Compared to the Western Disney theme parks, tickets here are relatively cheap.

You can purchase one-park or two-park tickets for one or multiple days at the ticket booths and online. TDR calls its tickets 'passports'.

The easiest place to buy the tickets (up to 3 months in advance) is the official website at tokyodisneyresort.jp. Tickets must be printed – barcodes are not accepted on smartphones. The website, bizarrely, closes between 3:00 am and 5:00 am (Japan Time) daily – you cannot buy tickets between these times. You can buy same-day tickets on the website if they are available.

You can also buy tickets at Disney Stores in Japan, major convenience stores, and JR ticket windows. If you insist on buying tickets on the day, arrive at least 45 minutes before park opening as ticket booths and ticket vending machines open 30 minutes before the park's opening time.

Finally, if you are staying at a Disney hotel, then you can buy the tickets at the hotel itself when you arrive, paying with either cash or card. You will be guaranteed entry to the parks and have additional ticket choices not available elsewhere.

You can make changes to tickets for ¥200, including changing the date and park.

Standard Ticket Prices:

1-Day Passport
Adult (Ages 18+): ¥7,500 (~$69/£53/€62)
Senior (Ages 65+): ¥6,800 (~$62/£48/€56)
Junior (Ages 12-17): ¥6,500 (~ $59/£46/€53)
Children (Ages 4-11): ¥4,900 (~$45/£34/€40)

2-Day Passport
Adult (Ages 18+): ¥13,400 (~$122/£94/€110)
Junior (Ages 12-17): ¥11,800 (~$108/£83/€97)
Children (Ages 4-11): ¥8,800 (~$80/£62/€73)

3-Day Passport
Adult (Ages 18+): ¥18,100 (~$165/£127/€149)
Junior (Ages 12-17): ¥15,800 (~$144/£111/€130)
Children (Ages 4-11): ¥11,800 (~$108/£83/€97)

4-Day Passport
Adult (Ages 18+): ¥22,800 (~$208/£160/€188)
Junior (Ages 12-17): ¥19,800 (~$181/£139/€163)
Children (Ages 4-11): ¥14,800 (~$135/£104/€122)

Other Tickets

There are two further tickets which may be unfamiliar to most people. These allow access to one park in the afternoon, or evening, without paying for a full day.

These tickets are not necessarily offered every day of the year, and will not be offered during very peak times. You can check in advance which tickets will be sold online at TDR's official website calendar - bit.ly/tdrcalendar2

After 6 Passport
Per Person: ¥4,300 (approx. $39/£30/€35)

This ticket is valid after 6:00 pm on weekdays (excluding public holidays) for entry into either park.

Starlight Passport
Per Person: ¥5,500 (approx. $50/£39/€45)

This ticket is valid after 3:00 pm on weekends and public holidays for entry into either park.

Natsu 5 Passport (Summer Only)
This ticket replaces the 'After 6 Passport' during a part of the summer, and allows access to either park on weekdays from 5:00 pm. It is usually priced at a similar price to the After 6 Passport.

Ticket Validity

1-Day and 2-Day tickets bought at the theme parks or online only allow access to one theme park per day. You can choose which park you will visit on each day, and can visit the same park on two days if you would like. With 3-Day and 4-Day tickets, on the first and second day, you will be limited to one park per day, but on the third and fourth day, you can visit both parks.

If you want to visit more than one park per day with a 1-Day or 2-Day, then you will need to stay at a Tokyo Disney Hotel and buy the tickets from the hotel counter (more details follow).

Children under 3 enter for free – proof of age may be requested.

Ticket prices last increased in October 2019.

Multi-Day Passport Specials

Guests staying at the four Disney hotels: MiraCosta Hotel, Tokyo Disneyland Hotel, Ambassador Hotel, and Tokyo Disney Celebration Hotel can buy exclusive tickets at the hotels which allow park-hopping from day 1. These tickets will enable you to go between Tokyo Disneyland Park and Tokyo DisneySea as you please on all days that your ticket is valid.

These tickets cost an additional ¥1,600 per adult, ¥1,200 per junior, and ¥1,000 per child more than the standard multi-day tickets on the previous page.

Whether you really need to be able to park-hop from day 1 is something you will need to decide on. There is certainly enough to do in each park to fill at least one full day in each. The layout of the resort also makes park-hopping lengthy: parks are built 'back to back,' so the main entrances of each theme park are on the complete opposite sides of the resort from each other and require a ride on the monorail or a long walk.

Understanding the Parks

Before taking a detailed look at each of the theme parks, we think it is best to explain some of the services on offer at each park, including Fastpass, Single Rider queue lines, and more.

When to Visit

Crowds at Tokyo Disney Resort vary significantly from season to season and even day to day. The difference in a single day can save you thousands of yen and hours in queue lines. You need to consider national and school holidays in Japan and surrounding countries, the weather, pricing, and more to find the best time to go.

If there is a specific attraction or show you wish to enjoy, be sure to check Tokyo Disney Resort's list of closures, which is published six months in advance - bit.ly/scheduletdr - each ride is closed at some point in the year for refurbishment, so bear this in mind.

Major Holidays (Times to Avoid) In 2020
• 1st to 5th January: New Year's Day & School Break
• 13th January: Coming of Age Day
• 11th February: National Foundation Day
• 23rd and 24th February: Emperor's Birthday
• 20th March: Vernal Equinox Day
• 21st March to 5th April: School Holidays
• 26th April to 9th May: Showa Day and Golden Week
• 23rd July to 10th August: 2020 Olympic Games and surrounding Holidays

• 13th to 15th August: Obon Week
• End of July to End of August: School Summer Holidays (30 to 40 days)
• 19th to 22nd September: Respect for the Aged Day and Autumnal Equinox Day (4-Day Weekend)
• 3rd November: Culture Day
• 23rd November: Labor Thanksgiving Day
• 19th December 2020 to 4th January 2021 - Christmas Holidays.

Ideal times to visit are, therefore: most of January and February, June, September, November to mid-December. Watch out for any holidays above, though.

Top Tip: If a public holiday falls on a Friday or a Monday, that weekend becomes an extended weekend. If it is on a Thursday or Tuesday, some people turn this into a 4-day

weekend. Avoid these extended weekends; they are always very busy.

Crowd Insight: In 2020, Tokyo hosts the Olympic Games from Friday, 24th July to Sunday, 9th August. The Paralympic Games will run from Tuesday, 25th August to Sunday, 6th September 2020. Although most people visiting Japan during this time will not visit Tokyo Disney Resort, some people will. This will cause marginally higher crowds in 2020. An even more significant effect will be the opening of several new rides in April 2020; for many visitors, the summer will be their first opportunity to visit these. We recommend you avoid the July to September period this year.

Days of the Week:
The days of the week that you visit make a huge difference to how long you will wait to get on rides. A

ride can have a wait time of 90 minutes on one day, and just 30 minutes the next. The most notable difference is between weekends and weekdays.

Crowd Calendar

As well as the above information to guide your visit, there is a fantastic online calendar available at bit.ly/tdrcrowds. This is not an official Disney calendar but instead uses several data sources to predict the crowds – we have found it to be very accurate and helpful in picking specific days to visit the parks – these are just predictions, however. The calendar is entirely in Japanese, but here we explain how to decipher it.

You should try and avoid days on the calendar which show the number of people with the color-coding of black, brown, red, or peach. The best colors are white, then blue, green and yellow. Looking at the numbers, the lower, the better.

Next, if you click on any date, you will see another screen that gives you information on the maximum expected standby wait times for top attractions, and then what times Fastpasses are expected to be available. We also include our own Fastpass availability projections in the Fastpass Availability section of this guide – feel free to use both. These are estimates, of course. Here is how to read these estimates.

The best day of the week to visit is usually Tuesday, then Wednesday, then Thursday, Friday, Monday, and Sunday - the busiest day of the week is by far Saturday. Park hours may be extended on weekends to compensate for larger crowds. Avoid weekends throughout the year unless this is your only way to visit.

Choose Your Options: Disneyland (Pink) or DisneySea (Blue). Tick the box in the green section to show Hotel Occupancy

Pick a Date: The dropdown with '1' lets you select how many months to show from today. The current year and month is shown, e.g. 2020年 1月 here means January 2020. You can go go back a month by pressing the white button to the left of the date, and go forward by pressing the button to the right.

Read the Crowd Calendar: From left to right are columns with days of the week, with Sunday on the left (日) and Saturday on the right (土). For each date you will see a square like this one on the right. The date is in big at the top, in this case it is '5', the 5th of January. Then you see two numbers under a sun symbol, these are the predicted maximum and minimum temperature in degrees celcius. In green underneath that is the park operating hours. Then the most crucial part is the number on the right - '55' in this case. This is the number of people expected in the park (in this case, 55000). If possible, try to visit on days where the number is under 35 for the best experience. The darker the color, and the higher the number, the larger the crowds.

Tokyo Disneyland						
スタンバイ・FP目安						
モンイン	プー	スプラ	バズ	ビッグ	スペ	ホンテ
SB (MAX)	120 | 180	120 | 180	120 | 180	120 | 150	120 | 150	120 | 150	90 | 120
08:00	10:00	09:00	09:00	10:00	09:00	09:00	09:00
09:00	18:00	16:00	14:00	14:00	12:00	11:00	10:00
10:00	-	20:00	19:00	19:00	15:00	13:00	11:00
11:00	-	-	-	19:00	15:00	14:00	
12:00	-	-	-	-	18:00	19:00	
13:00	-	-	-	-	20:00	-	
14:00	-	-	-	-	-		
15:00	-	-	-	-			
16:00	-	-	-				
17:00	-	-					
18:00	-						
19:00							
20:00							
21:00							

From left to right, the attractions listed here are:
- Monster's Inc., Ride and Go Seek (モンイン)
- Pooh's Hunny Hunt (プー)
- Splash Mountain (スプラ)
- Buzz Lightyear's Astro Blasters (バズ)
- Big Thunder Mountain (ビッグ)
- Space Mountain (スペ)
- Haunted Mansion (ホンテ)

Tokyo DisneySea						
スタンバイ・FP目安						
トイス	TOT	センター	インディ	レイジ	ストム	2万
SB (MAX)	150 | 300	90 | 150	120 | 180	90 | 180	90 | 150	45 | 120	60 | 120
08:00	12:00	09:00	09:00	09:00	09:00	09:00	09:00
09:00	-	16:00	11:00	11:00	10:00	10:00	10:00
10:00	-	19:00	14:00	14:00	11:00	11:00	11:00
11:00	-	-	17:00	17:00	13:00	12:00	12:00
12:00	-	-	20:00	20:00	15:00	13:00	13:00
13:00	-	-	-	-	18:00	15:00	14:00
14:00	-	-	-	-	20:00	17:00	15:00
15:00	-	-	-	-	-	19:00	17:00
16:00	-	-	-	-	-	20:00	19:00
17:00	-	-	-	-			20:00
18:00	-	-	-				
19:00	-	-					
20:00	-						
21:00							

From left to right, the attractions listed here are:
- Toy Story Mania (トイス)
- Tower of Terror (TOT)
- Journey to the Center of the Earth (センター)
- Indiana Jones Adventure (インディ)
- Raging Spirits (レイジ)
- Nemo & Friends SeaRider (ストム)
- 20,000 Leagues Under the Sea (2万)

We have included the Japanese character translation as this screen will likely change in the coming months to include the new FP-enabled attractions opening in 2020. At the time of writing, this website does not yet provide predictions for Soaring.

Fastpass

The Tokyo Disney Resort offers a unique skip-the-queue system called Fastpass *at no cost*. It allows you to reserve a time slot for certain attractions, return at an appointed time, and ride with little to no wait. While waiting for your Fastpass reservation time, you can do something else such as shop, dine, watch a show or experience another attraction.

How to use Fastpass

1. Find a Fastpass ride
You can identify rides that offer Fastpass (FP) by the FP logo on park maps. It is helpful to know which attractions offer Fastpass in advance by reading through this guide and looking at park maps.

2. Check the wait time and decide
At a FP-enabled attraction, there are two ride entrances – the standby entrance where you can queue up and ride (e.g., 45-minute wait), and the Fastpass entrance.

If the standby wait time is short, use the regular standby entrance. If the wait is too long for you, you should use the FP system.

If the standby wait is less than 30 minutes, we recommend waiting in the standby queue; this is because FastPasses often require you to backtrack across the park negating time savings.

3. Get your Fastpass
Near the ride entrance is the FP distribution area with machines and a screen showing the current 1-hour return time for FP reservations (e.g., 14:15 to 15:15). This is the time your reservation is made for and is printed on FPs.

Go to the FP machines and scan the QR code on your park ticket or annual pass.

The machine will print a paper FP reminder telling you the time of your reservation. This is the same as that shown on the screen above this Fastpass distribution area.

Keep your FP reminder and park ticket safe. Your FP reminder will be written both in Japanese and English.

4. Wait
Dine, explore the park, or enjoy another ride or show until your FP return time.

5. Return and Ride
Return to the ride during the time window on your FP, entering through the ride's Fastpass entrance. At the FastPass ride entrance, scan your park entrance ticket at the reader.

Unlike some other Disney theme parks, you do not need to hand over your FastPass Reminder slip and can keep this as a souvenir.

Later in the queue, you may need to scan your park ticket a second time on another reader.

Now, you can ride within a few minutes, skipping the regular queue – the wait time with a Fastpass is often under 10 minutes, but can be up to 15 minutes.

The Fastpass System Explained

Now that you have read about the advantages of the Fastpass system, we have to tell you the system's limitations - namely that you cannot use Fastpasses to avoid every single wait.

Firstly, not every ride offers Fastpass - only 8 (soon to be 10) rides out of 25 in Tokyo Disneyland offer this service, and in Tokyo DisneySea, it is 10 out of 22.

Secondly, you can only hold one Fastpass ticket (and therefore only skip one queue) at a time, though there are exceptions to this as noted on the next page.

Therefore, you will use Fastpass throughout your time at the Tokyo Disney Resort a limited number of times.

How Fastpass works:
Every Tokyo Disney Resort theme park entry ticket and annual pass includes Fastpass access – it is a free system open to every guest.

Each day, Cast Members will decide what percentage of riders they will be able to use the Fastpass system. Let's say that in this case, it is 50%.

So, assuming 2000 guests per hour can ride Big Thunder Mountain, the Fastpass system will distribute 1000 Fastpass tickets for each operating hour. This means 50% of

guests will use Fastpass to board the ride, and 50% will use the standby queue each hour.

There are, therefore, a limited number of Fastpass tickets for each ride each hour. This is to ensure that the standby queue line is kept to a reasonable level.

The first Fastpass return time for an attraction is usually 30 minutes after park opening, although sometimes it is later.

Fastpass slots then move in 5-minute increments, so after all the Fastpasses for 10:30 am-11:30 am are distributed, the next return time will be 10:35 am-11:35 am.

Once all Fastpasses have been distributed for the day, the ticket distribution machines are shut down.

Rides may not offer Fastpasses for the entire park operating hours for a variety of reasons.

If you want to know the time of the last Fastpass return, ask the Cast Members at the attraction. When Fastpass stops being used, the regular queue usually moves twice as quickly.

On occasion, towards the end of the day, the standard standby queue may not be available, and only those

holding FastPass reservations may ride.

Due to the limited number of Fastpasses available, tickets often run out on popular rides early in the day. This happens regularly on *Pooh's Hunny Hunt, Monsters Inc. Ride & Go Seek!, Soaring: Fantastic Flight, Toy Story Mania!, Tower of Terror* and *Journey to the Center of the Earth.* When *Enchanted Tale of Beauty and the Beast* opens on 15th April 2020, we expect these FastPasses to disappear within an hour of park opening.

On busy days these rides will distribute their daily allocation of Fastpasses within 1-2 hours of park opening and sometimes within 30 minutes.

Is Fastpass always available?
Yes, this service is offered daily.

Good to Know:
Tower of Terror and *Soaring* both have a compulsory pre-show video even in the Fastpass queue. After this, you enter a short queue line to board the ride vehicle itself, but the wait may be up to 15 minutes.

On other attractions, you should be on the ride in less than ten minutes after arriving with a Fastpass.

Digital FastPass: The Spanner in the Works!

In Summer 2019, Tokyo Disney Resort revolutionized the Fastpass system by introducing a digital Fastpass system. This way, instead of crisscrossing the park, scanning your park ticket, and getting a Fastpass reminder and reservation, you can simply open an app and reserve a Fastpass from anywhere in the park. Reservations are made on the day in the app.

The only problem is that the app is only available in Japanese app stores, and is also only available in the Japanese language. If you are prepared to put in the effort to create a new iTunes account with a Japanese address, create a Tokyo Disney Resort account, scan the ticket, and follow step by step instructions, then you too can be a member of this exclusive club. Android users have it slightly easier as they won't need to create a new Japanese account to download the app.

We can only hope that in the future, the app will be translated into English and be available internationally. Until then, if you are up for the challenge, we recommend you follow this post on TouringPlans.com, which has detailed instructions - http://bit.ly/japanfp.

The paper Fastpass system is still available, and we have had no issues riding everything we wanted using either system.

Get Extra Fastpasses

Officially, you can only hold one Fastpass at a time, but, there are exceptions.
• When your Fastpass return time starts, you can get another Fastpass even if you have not used your current Fastpass yet. E.g., You have a Star Tours Fastpass for 14:00-15:00. You can get another Fastpass from 14:00.
• Cast Members (at their discretion) may allow you to use a Fastpass after the return time, although not before. In Japan, it is considered rude to be late, but if you have a valid reason (such as a ride breakdown or overrunning meal), Cast Members may accommodate this.
• The Fastpass system is not connected between the two theme parks. Therefore, you can hold a Fastpass for a Tokyo Disneyland ride and another for a Tokyo DisneySea ride at the same time. However, it can take 30 minutes from one park to the other, including the time to ride the monorail. You must have a ticket which allows you to enter both parks on the same day. We do not suggest doing this, but it is possible.
• If your return time is over two hours away, you can get a second Fastpass two hours after picking up the first. E.g., You got a *Soaring* Fastpass reservation at 10:00; the return time is 15:00-16:00. As 15:00 is over two hours away from when you got your Fastpass reservation, you can get another Fastpass reservation at noon (two hours after 10:00). Check the time your next Fastpass is available at the bottom of your latest Fastpass reminder ticket.

Fastpass Attractions List

Tokyo Disneyland Park:
• Big Thunder Mountain
• Splash Mountain
• Pooh's Hunny Hunt
• Haunted Mansion
• Enchanted Tale of Beauty and the Beast (starting 15th April 2020)
• The Happy Ride with Baymax (starting 15th April 2020)
• Star Tours: The Adventures Continue
• Space Mountain
• Buzz Lightyear's Astro Blasters
• Monsters, Inc. Ride & Go Seek!

Tokyo DisneySea:
• Soaring: Fantastic Flight
• Tower of Terror
• Toy Story Mania!
• Nemo & Friends SeaRider
• Indiana Jones Adventure: Temple of the Crystal Skull
• Raging Spirits
• The Magic Lamp Theater
• Mermaid Lagoon Theater
• 20,000 Leagues Under the Sea
• Journey to the Center of the Earth

Fastpass Availability

Not every Fastpass is created equal – there are some attractions which are more popular than others, some attractions distribute most Fastpasses than others, and some Fastpasses will save you more time than others.

Here we cover on average how quickly Fastpasses end distribution for the day for each attraction. Once Fastpasses have been allocated for the whole day, the only way to experience the attraction without a Fastpass is to use the lengthy standby queue line, so you should priorities Fastpasses for attractions that run out of Fastpasses earlier in the day.

To use this section, firstly, you will need to use the Japanese crowd calendar at bit.ly/tdrcrowds to see how busy the park is expected to be on the dates of your visit. Next, match the color below from that calendar for an idea of what time Fastpasses are likely to run out for attractions based on a park opening time of 8:00 am and closing time of 10:00 pm. Move these times forward or backward by one hour if the park opening hours are different during your visit.

These estimates are based on historical data, but the parks are always changing, and with the addition of two new rides with Fastpass in 2020, Fastpass availability may well increase for the better.

Tokyo Disneyland

	Empty (white)	Reasonably Empty	Some Crowds		Somewhat Crowded	Crowded	Very Crowded	Severe Crowds
Big Thunder Mountain	20:15-20:45	15:45-16:15	13:15-15:15	11:45-14:15	11:45-12:15	11:45	11:45	11:00
Splash Mountain	18:00-18:30	13:45-14:45	12:15-14:15	10:45-13:45	10:45-11:15	10:15	09:45	09:30
Pooh's Hunny Hunt	15:15-16:15	12:15-13:45	11:30-12:45	10:45-11:45	10:45-11:15	10:45-11:15	09:15	08:30-09:00
Haunted Mansion	20:45-21:15	17:00-19:00	15:00-17:00	12:15-15:15	12:45-13:15	12:45-13:15	13:15	12:00
Beauty & the Beast (opens 15th Apr 2020)	11:00-12:00 (est)	10:00-11:00 (est)	09:45-10:30 (est)	09:30-10:00 (est)	09:00-09:30 (est)	08:20-09:00 (est)	08:15 - 08:30 (est.)	08:10 - 08:20 (est.)
Baymax (opens 15th Apr 2020)	18:00-20:00 (est)	15:45 (est.)	14:00 (est)	12:45 (est)	12:15 (est)	11:45-12:15 (est)	10:45 (est)	10:15
Star Tours (FP issuance may start late)	21:15 - May not issue FP	21:15 - May not issue FP	18:00 - May not issue FP	15:45	14:15-15:15	13:15-14:45	12:45-13:45	12:00-13:00
Space Mountain	20:00-20:30	17:00-18:00	15:15-16:00	13:15-14:00	11:45-12:15	11:30-12:00	11:15-11:45	10:45-11:45
Buzz Lightyear's Astro Blasters	18:15-18:45	14:45-15:45	13:30-14:30	12:30-13:00	11:45-12:15	11:30-12:15	10:30-11:30	10:15-11:00
Monsters Inc., Ride & Go Seek	14:15-15:15	12:15-13:15	12:00-13:00	11:45-12:45	10:15-12:15	10:00-10:45	09:00-09:45	08:30-09:15

It's clear that the priorities for Fastpasses should be *Enchanted Tale of Beauty and the Beast*, *Pooh's Hunny Hunt* and *Monsters Inc. Ride & Go Seek*. It is unlikely you will be able to get more than one of these in any one day during busier times of the year.

Tokyo DisneySea

	Empty (white)	Reasonably Empty	Some Crowds		Somewhat Crowded	Crowded	Very Crowded	Severe Crowds
Soaring: Fantastic Flight	10:00-11:00	09:00-09:45	08:35-09:10	08:30-09:00	08:30-08:45	08:20-08:30	08:15-08:25	08:10-08:20
Tower of Terror	16:15-17:15	15:15-16:45	13:45-15:45	12:15-14:15	13:45-15:15	10:45-11:00	10:15-11:00	09:45-11:00
Toy Story Mania!	10:45-12:45	10:00-10:15	09:30-10:15	08:45-10:15	08:45-09:45	09:00-09:15	08:30-09:45	08:15-08:30
Nemo & Friends	21:15	17:15-21:15	16:30-21:15	15:45-21:15	14:30-16:45	12:45-13:15	12:15	11:15
Indiana Jones	19:45	14:45-19:45	14:00-16:00	13:45-14:15	12:15-14:15	13:00-14:00	10:15-10:45	10:00-10:30
Raging Spirits	19:45-20:45	14:45-20:45	14:00-18:00	13:45-14:45	13:15-14:45	11:45-12:15	10:45-12:15	11:15
Magic Lamp Theater	20:45	20:45	18:00-20:45	17:15-20:45	15:45-18:45	14:15	13:15-13:45	12:15
20,000 Leagues	21:15	21:15	21:15	21:15	15:45-21:15	15:15-15:45	13:45-14:15	12:15
Journey to the Center of the Earth	14:45-18:45	16:45	15:30	12:15	10:45-12:45	10:45-11:15	09:45-10:15	09:30-10:15

At Tokyo DisneySea, *Soaring* dominates as the most important Fastpass to get, with Fastpasses running out within 10 minutes on the very busiest of days, and within 2-3 hours even on the emptiest days. *Toy Story Mania!* follows in a close second, followed by *Journey to the Center of the Earth* and *Tower of Terror.* You should be able to get a Fastpass for either *Soaring* or *Toy Story Mania* first thing, and then a second

Fastpass for *Journey* or *Tower* on all but the very busiest of days.

Mermaid Lagoon Theater generally allows you to get a Fastpass for a show in the next 15 to 45 minutes. If the wait time is short, use the standby queue instead of wasting a Fastpass – the exception is if you have kids who want to experience the rides in Mermaid Lagoon while you wait for your Fastpass time for the show.

On days labeled above as *empty, reasonably empty* and *some crowds*, some attractions (such as *Star Tours*) may not operate Fastpass at all, or may only offer Fastpass for a period of the day, after which the ride will be accessible via the standby queue only. This usually happens when Fastpass is not providing time savings, so you can join the line and ride within less than 20 minutes.

On-Ride Photos

Some of Tokyo Disney Resort's rides have cameras positioned and timed to take perfect on-ride photos of you at the fastest, steepest, scariest, and most fun moments. These make for timeless keepsakes.

When you get off selected rides, you will walk past screens that preview your photo (with a watermark on

top). If you wish to buy it, go to the photo counter.

You do not have to buy on-ride photos straight after your ride; you can pick them up at any time that same day. Just remember your unique number at the ride exit or ask a member of staff at the photo kiosk to write it down for you.

If you like the photo, Cast Members will show it to you up close before you pay for it. If you like it, buy it! You will treasure the photo for a long time.

Attractions with on-ride photos are *Splash Mountain, Tower of Terror,* and *Indiana Jones Adventure: Temple of the Crystal Skull.*

Tokyo Disney Resort App

The Tokyo Disney Resort has a free Apple iOS and Android app to enhance your trip. You can check opening hours, show and parade times, attraction wait times, plus make digital Fastpass reservations, making the app very useful.

You will need a data connection, which means you must have data roaming enabled on your phone.

Data usage is minimal for the app, but it may likely cost you if you are not from Japan. We recommend a Japanese sim card as per our earlier chapters. There is Free Wi-Fi in the park near the entrance but not around the rest of the parks, making this fairly useless.

You must have a Japanese iTunes account to download the app on Apple devices. Android users from any country can download the app. The app is only in Japanese. We hope that in the future, the app will be translated into English and be available internationally.

Until then, if you are up for the challenge, follow this post on TouringPlans.com with detailed instructions - www.bit.ly/japanfp.

If you only want to see the wait times, showtimes, and current FastPass distribution times (but not book Fastpass), then tokyodisneyresort.jp has all this information and is available via your mobile browser. Tap the button either for Tokyo Disneyland or Tokyo DisneySea at the top, then 'Today.'

Doing Disney on a Budget

A visit to Tokyo Disney Resort is pricey. However, there are ways to reduce your spending at the resort and still have a magical time.

1. Hotels – Disney hotels are themed, have early park entry and other benefits but are also much more expensive than other nearby hotels, such as those on the monorail loop. These are in a great location, but are a fraction of the price.

2. Eat at Ikspiari – Ikspiari is a giant entertainment complex located on Disney property near the resort's entrance. The food here is substantially cheaper than the food in the theme parks. See our Ikspiari section for more details.

3. Take your own photos – If you do not want to pay for an 'official' Disney character photo, take one yourself; the Cast Members do not mind. They will even take the photo for you!

4. Take your own gifts – Buy dresses, outfits, and toys outside of Tokyo Disney from Disney Stores, online, or at supermarkets before you visit the resort. Give your child the costume on arrival to avoid the high in-park merchandise prices. The Disney Store in Shibuya (Tokyo) has a discounted section on the top floor.

5. More affordable meals – Although food prices are high, some restaurants offer better value than others, such as *China Voyager* or *Dockside Diner*. Try the set menus or a buffet as a late lunch and a lighter dinner. Also, don't buy a whole set menu – most items can be purchased individually.

6. Park Tickets – We recommend you purchase your tickets in advance. You can either do this at the official Tokyo Disney Resort website or from other retailers. During quieter periods, you may find slightly discounted tickets available on the website – usually with a small saving of ¥500 per person, but this adds up for a group. Also, many convenience stores (such as 7 Eleven or Family Mart) in Tokyo sell tickets from a vending machine throughout the year at a slight discount of around ¥500 per ticket.

7. Take Snacks – According to park rules, you are requested not to bring in external food or drink. However, this isn't enforced, although we have been asked not to eat snacks at security. You should officially consume any food in the picnic areas outside the park – whether you do that is up to you. At the very least, take a bottle of water in with you (which *is* allowed) – there are water fountains in both parks to refill throughout the day.

Rider Switch

Rider Switch is a time-saving solution that allows parents to reduce queuing times throughout their visit when riding thrill attractions.

A common issue at theme parks is when two adults want to ride a thrill ride, but they have a child who is not tall enough to ride. There are three solutions:

a) the adults can take turns to ride (queuing twice);
b) one adult can choose not to experience the attraction; c) skip the attraction.

The solution is Disney's Rider Switch, which allows one adult to queue up and ride while the other stays with the child.

When the first adult reaches the end of the queue line, they ask for a Rider Switch pass. The second adult is then able to ride as soon as the first one returns. The second adult is granted almost immediate access to the ride, usually through the exit, bypassing the entire regular queue line. Each adult will experience the ride separately, but the second adult will not need to wait to ride.

Each attraction implements the system in a slightly different manner, so ask Cast Members at ride entrances for details.

Single Rider

One of the best ways to significantly reduce your time waiting for attractions is to use the Single Rider queue instead of the regular standby queue. This is available at selected attractions at the resort.

The Single Rider queue fills free spaces on ride vehicles. For example, if a ride vehicle can seat 8 people and a group of 4 turns up, followed by a group of 3, then a Single Rider will fill the free space.

This allows guests who are willing to ride with strangers to experience a shorter wait, and fills a space. This system reduces waits for all.

Single Rider queues may be closed when waits in that queue are too long, or when the theme park is not busy.

Single Rider Lines can be used by groups too, but members of the group will be separated, and each will ride in a different vehicle. You can, of course, wait for each other after riding by the exit but you will not ride together.

The following attractions operate Single Rider Lines:

• Splash Mountain
• Indiana Jones Adventure: Temple of the Crystal Skull
• Raging Spirits
• The Enchanted Tale of Beauty and the Beast (from April 2020)

To use Single Rider simply ask the Cast Member at the ride entrance, they will direct you to a separate queue line and give you a Single Rider ticket, which you will need to hand to a Cast Member at the end of the queue. You may also be directed to the Fastpass queue instead and be given this same Single Rider ticket.

We have found that Single Rider works particularly well on saving time on *Indiana Jones Adventure* and *Splash Mountain* as Japanese guests seem to want to ride together and not alone. However, on *Raging Spirits* as the ride capacity is low and the rows are of 2 people, it is rarer to find a free space and the Single Rider queue is not as effective – we still found that we saved 50-80% of queuing time using this technique, however, on all three rides.

Early Park Entry – Happy15

Happy15 allows guests staying at the four Disney hotels (Hotel MiraCosta, Disneyland Hotel, Ambassador Hotel, and Tokyo Disney Celebration Hotel) early theme park access to selected attractions at both theme parks at the Tokyo Disney Resort for 15 minutes each morning. Guests get access to an almost empty park, ride with little to no wait, and, importantly, can get in a queue for FastPasses for popular rides. Fifteen minutes may not sound like much, but this little benefit can really improve your enjoyment of the theme parks in setting you up for a fantastic day and skipping one or two long waits for rides.

Happy15 usually takes place at both theme parks daily. Check the Tokyo Disney Resort website for details.

Using 'Happy15'
Disney hotel guests will need their park tickets and their Happy15 voucher (one voucher given at check-in per person per day) and park entry ticket. The Happy15 voucher will be collected near the park entrance at Tokyo DisneySea. At Tokyo Disneyland Park, the voucher will be collected either at the park entrance or on peak days within specified areas in the park after the covered World Bazaar area.

Only the four Disney hotels mentioned above offer this early access privilege, not the Official, Partner, or Good Neighbor Hotels.

What is open during Happy15?
The content of Happy15 changes regularly.

At the time of writing, at Tokyo Disneyland Park, *Buzz Lightyear's Astro Blasters* is available during this time. Between 25th February and 3rd March 2020, the available attraction will be changed to *Monsters Inc. Ride & Go Seek!* From 15th April 2020, the available attraction will be changed to *Enchanted Tale of Beauty and the Beast.*

Meanwhile, at Tokyo DisneySea, at the time of writing *Toy Story Mania!* and *Soaring: Fantastic Flight* are both available during Happy15. Between 11th May and 29th June 2020, the available attractions will be changed to *Soaring: Fantastic Flight* and *Tower of Terror.*

This page contains details of current Happy15 attractions - http://bit.ly/happy15tdr.

Future Changes
Happy 15 Entry is available during your stay on days other than the check-in day.

(However, Guests staying at Disney Ambassador Hotel and Tokyo DisneySea Hotel MiraCosta will be allowed early entry to Tokyo DisneySea Park even on their check-in day).

The following changes will be made to Happy 15 Entry starting 1st June 2020.

• For guests staying at Tokyo DisneySea Hotel MiraCosta, Happy 15 Entry will only be available from the second day of your stay onwards (and no longer on check-in day).

• For guests staying at Tokyo Disney Celebration Hotel, Happy 15 Entry will only be available for Tokyo Disneyland Park.

Guided Tours

Note: These tours are only offered in Japanese.

If you want to discover more about the magic behind Tokyo Disney Resort's two theme parks, be sure to join one of the resort's guided tours. Led by a Guest Relations Cast Member, these tours are the perfect way to enhance your visit.

Each park tour lasts for 90 minutes. You will discover the work that goes into creating these parks. You will find out secrets and notice details that will make you stop and say, "wow." The tour is available in Japanese only.

Pricing for each theme park tour is ¥2,500 for adults and juniors, and ¥1,000 per child.

Reservations can be made online at https://reserve.tokyodisney resort.jp/guidetour/list/.

Stroller and Wheelchair Rental

Wheelchair and stroller rentals are available for guests who do not wish to bring their own.

If your child is recently out of a stroller, it is often still worth renting one as it is likely they will get tired, due to the vast walking distances involved with a Tokyo Disney Resort visit.

Sometimes it is nice just to let kids sit in their pushchair and have a break. They can also be used as an easy way to carry around bags.

The daily cost of hiring a stroller is ¥1,000. A standard wheelchair costs ¥500 for the day, whereas a motorized wheelchair costs ¥2,000, and a battery-assisted push wheelchair is ¥1,000 per day.

You are, of course, welcome to bring your own stroller or wheelchair if you wish.

When experiencing attractions, be sure to leave your stroller in the dedicated parking areas. Ask a Cast Member if you are not sure whether this is.

Strollers may be moved by Cast Members to keep them neat and organized.

Lockers

There are coin-operated lockers available both inside and outside the theme parks.

At Tokyo DisneySea, there are two locker locations just after the park turnstiles. There are a further six locations outside the park turnstiles, including at the Tokyo DisneySea Disney Resort Line monorail station. The same applies to Tokyo Disneyland with two locations just after the park turnstiles and six other sites just outside the park entrance, including at Tokyo Disneyland Station on the Disney Resort Line monorail.

Locker fees are:
• Super-Extra Large - ¥800
• Extra Large - ¥800
• Large (carry-on size) - ¥600
• Medium - ¥500
• Small - ¥400

Additionally, at JR Maihama station, you will find lockers of all different sizes. These lockers also take notes/bills and Suica/Pasmo transport cards used on the subway and JR lines, as well as coins.

Spend Less Time Waiting in Queue Lines

The Tokyo Disney Resort meticulously themes its queues to introduce an attraction's story before you board. However, no one likes waiting, and often you want to ride as quickly as possible. Remember that a visit to a theme park will involve waiting in queue lines; this chapter covers our top tips on minimizing these waits.

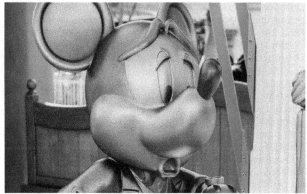

1. Eat outside the regular dining hours

At Tokyo Disney Resort, whether you want to eat at a Table Service restaurant or a Counter Service meal, waiting for your food is part of the game. Have lunch before midday or after 3:00 pm for much shorter waits. Also, having dinner before 7:00 pm will reduce your time waiting. Waits of 20 minutes or longer to order are relatively typical at peak times at Counter Service restaurants.

2. Counter Service meal tricks

At Counter Service locations, each cashier has two queues, and alternates between them – count how many groups (families or friends) are in front of you in the queue. There may be ten people in front of you in one queue line but only two families. The other queue line may have five people but from five different families. The queue with ten people will move more quickly with only two orders to process versus the other queue's five orders.

3. On-site Disney hotel guests

If you are staying at a Disney hotel at the Tokyo Disney Resort, take advantage of Happy15 early entry. You get admission into the theme parks fifteen minutes before regular guests do. Although this may not sound like much, using this time wisely will allow you to ride one popular attraction and get a Fastpass, saving you several hours straight away. See our Happy15 section for more details.

4. Get to the parks before opening time

If the park opens at 9:00 am, you should be at the park entrance at least 30 minutes before so that you can be as close to the front of the queue as possible. The same applies to Happy15 entry, get there about 15 minutes early to be as close to the front as possible. On peak days and weekends, add 15 minutes to these times.

5. Use FastPass and Single Rider

Earlier in this section, we covered the Fastpass system in detail. This is a free system, and you must use it to minimize waits effectively. You should be able to get at least 3 Fastpasses each day through proper planning. See our chapter entitled 'Touring Plans' for more details on how to maximize your time at the park. Plus, you can also use the Single Rider queue line to save a lot of time (we also covered that in detail earlier in this chapter).

6. Skip the parades and fireworks

If you have already seen the parades, shows, or fireworks, use that time to experience rides as the wait times are often shorter during these big events – this mainly applies to the nighttime spectaculars and the daytime parade. If you have not seen the park's entertainment offerings before, we recommend you watch these. Parades and shows are only performed at set times of the day, and most of these are as good as, if not better than, many rides.

7. Ride outdoor attractions when it rains
Outdoor attractions such as Dumbo, Splash Mountain (partially outdoor), Big Thunder Mountain, and Raging Spirits often have significantly reduced waits when it is raining. Yes, you may get wet while riding (a jacket will help), but the wait times will be shorter. In contrast, avoid the indoor rides when there is inclement weather as the waits will be artificially longer.

8. Choose when to visit
Visit during an off-peak time if possible. If you are visiting on New Year's Day, expect to queue a lot longer than in the middle of February. Of course, weekends are busier than weekdays. See our 'When to Visit' section to make the most of your time.

9. Shop at the end of the day
Go shopping at the end of the day. Even when the park is 'officially' closed, the shops by the park entrance areas stay open longer than the rest of the park. Alternatively, go to Ikspiari in the evening or your hotel's Disney shop, which are all open late.

Shop at strategic times, and make the most of your time in the parks.

10. Get a Times Guide
Get your Park Map and the 'Today' Times Guide on the way in; you will usually find them distributed together. The 'Today' Times Guide lists all time-sensitive information at the parks such as the timings of parades, shows, character appearances, and more. As such, you will not waste time crossing the park to find out that a character you saw earlier in the day has now left a particular location.

Meeting the Characters

For many visitors, meeting characters is the highlight of their trip. Playing with Pluto, talking to Cinderella, and hugging Mickey makes for magical memories.

The Japanese love their Disney characters, particularly the Duffy family of characters, and will form very long queues very quickly. To reduce wait times, guests are asked to limit photos to just one per party when using their own camera.

Tokyo Disneyland:
Certain characters are scheduled to appear around the park throughout the day. Times for the following will appear on your park map.

Mickey and Minnie can be found at *World Bazaar* (park entrance area).

At *Woodchuck Greeting Trail* in *Westernland*, you will usually find Daisy and Donald Duck.

At *Mickey's House and Meet Mickey in Toontown*, you can meet Mickey Mouse in one of four different (random) outfits, including his classic Steamboat Mickey costume.

There are also many other random character meet and greets around the park for which timings are not published. Characters change regularly, and these are merely examples. Characters will be present in an area that is relevant to them and their setting. The characters generally meet in the morning and afternoon, but not evening or nighttime.

In *World Bazaar*, you will find classic Disney characters, including Snow White, The Seven Dwarves, Cinderella, Pinocchio, Rapunzel, Aurora (Sleeping Beauty), Chip 'n Dale, Goofy, Pluto, Mary Poppins, Eeyore, Tigger, Piglet, Alice (in Wonderland). The characters will meet under the covered roof section during inclement weather.

In *Adventureland*, you can often find Baloo, King Louie, and Jose Carioca.

In *Westernland*, you may find Woody, Jessie, Chip 'n Dale, Mickey and Minnie, and Donald and Daisy.

In *Critter Country*, regular characters include Br'er Rabbit, Br'er Bear, Br'er Fox, Pocahontas, and Chip 'n Dale.

In *Fantasyland*, you will find characters from classic

Disney films such as Cinderella and Prince Charming, Alice (in Wonderland), the Mad Hatter, Peter Pan, Captain Hook, Mr. Smee, Aurora (Sleeping Beauty), Mary Poppins and Bert, Gaston, and Belle. You may also see 'new classic' characters like Rapunzel.

In *Toontown*, you can see the classic comic book and Disney shorts characters, including Mickey, Minnie, Clarabelle Cow, Horace Horsecollar, Scrooge McDuck, Max, Donald, and Daisy.

In *Tomorrowland*, you may see Stitch, Mr. and Mrs. Incredible, and Star Wars' Stormtroopers.

If there is a specific character you would like to see, ask at Guest Relations whether they have a schedule for them. Not all characters are available to meet daily.

Tokyo DisneySea:
This park has four scheduled character meets every day.

At the *Village Greeting Place* in *Cape Cod*, you can meet Shellie May. At the *Saludos Amigos! Greeting Dock* in *Lost River Delta*, you can meet Duffy.

Ariel's Greeting Grotto in Mermaid Lagoon is, of course, the place to meet Ariel herself.

Finally, *Mickey & Friends' Greeting Trails* in *Lost River*

Delta, you will find Mickey and Minnie.

Many other random meet-and-greets are not announced on the park's 'Today' Times Guide. You will commonly see the following characters around the park.

At the *DisneySea Plaza* (park entrance) and *Mediterranean Harbor,* you can often meet classic characters such as Mickey, Minnie, Goofy, Pluto, Donald, Daisy, and Chip 'n Dale.

At *American Waterfront*, look out for Goofy, Jiminy Cricket, and Gepetto.

At *Port Discovery*, you may see Mr. and Mrs. Incredible, Chip 'n Dale, and Goofy.

At *Lost River Delta*, you could encounter Indiana Jones, Max, Chip 'n Dale,

Panchito and Jose Carioca.

Mermaid Lagoon is home to many characters such as Prince Eric, Goofy, Pluto, Donald, and Daisy.

Arabian Coast is home to characters from the Aladdin movies, including Jasmine, Aladdin, Abu, Jafar, and Genie.

Hotels:
Characters are present at the Disney Ambassador Hotel in Chef Mickey, a character dining buffet with both Western and Japanese options. It serves breakfast, lunch, and dinner.

Breakfast is exclusively for Guests staying at the Disney Ambassador Hotel, but everyone can eat here at lunch and dinner (reservations are recommended). There is a 1 hour 30-minute limit to the buffet.

Park Entertainment Rules and Etiquette

Tokyo Disney Resort has several rules and regulations regarding how to watch park entertainment, such as parades, shows, and nighttime spectaculars. These are in place to ensure everyone has the best experience.

Key points include:
• For everyone's safety when taking photos or videos, please refrain from using equipment such as monopods, tripods, or selfie sticks (hand-size grip attachments permitted).
• When viewing performances, please remove large hats or other headwear and do not raise cameras above head-level.
• Filming is not permitted on most rides and shows.
• Please fold strollers when viewing performances; this includes parades.

For outdoor shows and parades, there will be a designated seating area for watching the performance. Behind the seated guests, other guests may stand to view the performance. This means for parades, the first two or three rows will be for sitting on the floor only, and for shows, there may be a large sitting area (as in the image shown above). You may bring floor mats to stake out your spot up to one hour before each performance – you will see many guests with plastic sheets doing this (see photo).

Guests will happily wait an hour in the same spot for a show, so this is something to bear in mind if you like being right at the front – get there very early.

At Tokyo Disney, the guests are exceptionally polite and orderly, and it makes watching parades and shows much more pleasant than at any other Disney park; there is no pushing or shoving at all – we wish these policies would be adopted at Disney parks worldwide.

Tokyo Disney Resort Online Photo

You will need to ask an in-park photographer for a free photo card to use this service. You then reuse this same card throughout your stay each time you have a photo taken by Disney.

You can get photos with Disney characters in some locations, ride photos from three attractions (ask at the ride for the photo to be added to your photo card), and shots with park icons such as the Aquasphere at the entrance of Tokyo DisneySea or Cinderella Castle at Tokyo Disneyland.

Once you have all the photos for your stay, you can visit tdronlinephoto.jp and download the images. One picture is ¥490, five photos are ¥1,600, and 10 photos are ¥2,700, for example. The website is targeted at Japanese consumers who can get these photos added to a 'Snap Photo CD' or even printed as a photobook – shipping is to Japan only.

Alternatively, you can visit either Fotografica in Tokyo DisneySea or Camera Center in Tokyo Disneyland and create a 'Snap Photo CD' there with all the photos from your trip. Pricing is ¥4,600 for 1 to 10 photos, ¥5,800 for 11-30 photos, and ¥8,000 for 31-100 photos.

For single photos, you will be given a receipt with a code to redeem at photo print locations and will not need to use this system.

Tokyo Disney Resort also offers a feature called 'Digital Photo Express' which allows you to take park photos or even photos from your smartphone and add borders and 'stickers' on a screen – you can then have these printed for ¥55 to ¥1,100 per print depending on the size.

Ride Height Requirements

Certain attractions at both theme parks have minimum height requirements to ride for safety reasons. These are strict and are not bent for anyone – these height restrictions are here for safety and are set in stone.

To make the process easier, when visiting the first ride of the day, a Cast Member will measure your child and will issue them a wristband of a certain color, which indicates at a glance which rides your child can or cannot ride. On future rides, you show this wristband to the Cast Member without needing to remeasure each time. You can also get this wristband from a Cast Member at the park information boards, too.

Here we list all of the current ride height requirements for your easy reference.

Do remember that just because your child may meet the height requirement doesn't necessarily mean that they won't be scared of the ride, and vice-versa.

Tokyo Disneyland
- The Happy Ride with Baymax (81cm)
- Splash Mountain (90cm)
- Gadget's Go Coaster (90cm)
- Big Thunder Mountain (102cm)
- Star Tours: The Aventures Continue (102cm)
- Space Mountain (102cm)

Tokyo DisneySea
- Nemo & Friends Searider (90cm)
- Flounder's Flying Fish Coaster (90cm)
- Tower of Terror (102cm)
- Soaring: Fantastic Flight (102cm)
- Indiana Jones Adventure (117cm)
- Raging Spirits (117cm)
- Journey to the Center of the Earth (117cm)

Show Lotteries

To make sure that all guests have a fair chance at seeing the in-park shows, several shows throughout the park operate with a lottery ticket system; this means you must have a winning lottery ticket to see certain shows.

1. You will need to proceed to either Biglietteria in Tokyo DisneySea, or Tomorrowland Hall in Tokyo Disneyland. All ticket lotteries are done centrally at these locations.
2. Approach one of the kiosks. The machine operates in several languages, including English.
3. Choose the show you would like to see, followed by the time of the performance.
4. Scan all the tickets of those in your party who wish to watch a show. Confirm the number of scanned tickets is correct.
5. You are told on the next screen whether you have won seats for that show. If you have, you are given a receipt to present before showtime at the theater.

You may only attempt each lottery once per show (not per performance) per day. The system is completely random, and there does not seem to be a way to increase your chances of winning – ticket lotteries will stop for each show when all tickets are won, or 45 minutes before a performance.

The first performance of the day of each show is open to all guests on a standby basis only, as a lottery is not held. For all other performances, there will also be some space reserved for standby visitors as well as lottery winners – you will need to be at the show at least 30-60 minutes before for a standby seat.

On certain dates, no lotteries will be held – in this case, go directly to the theaters before showtime.

If you have more than one child aged 3 or under with you to view entertainment, please contact a Cast Member at the ticket lottery locations before attempting the lottery.

Tokyo Disneyland

The first park at the Tokyo Disney Resort is composed of seven lands filled with fantasy, adventure, and excitement.

Tokyo Disneyland, also known as Tokyo Disneyland Park, is based on the original Disneyland that opened in California in 1955. Every Disney resort around the world has one of these classic "Magic Kingdom-style" Disney parks. The park spans 114 acres, which is 50% larger than the original, and larger than the Magic Kingdom in Florida.

Tokyo Disneyland is the most visited theme park outside of the USA, and the third most visited in the world, with 17.9 million visitors in 2018. It comes only third to the Magic Kingdom in Florida, and Disneyland Park in California. The park has plenty to offer guests with over forty attractions (rides, themed areas, and shows), as well as character experiences, dining options, and an abundance of places to shop.

Tokyo Disneyland is, in our opinion, the best' Magic Kingdom'-style theme park in the world.

The park is divided into seven areas (or "lands") around Cinderella Castle in the center. These are World Bazaar (the equivalent to Main Street USA in other Disney parks), Adventureland, Westernland, Critter Country, Fantasyland, Toontown, and Tomorrowland. Each land has its own overarching theme, with its own soundtrack, décor, costumes, and themed attractions. Unlike many other Disney Magic Kingdom-style parks, there is no Disneyland Railroad around the park to transport guests between these different lands.

We will now take a look at each land individually, as well as the attractions, dining options, and other notable features.

	Does the attraction have Fastpass?		Minimum height (in cm)
	Is there an On-Ride Photo?		Attraction Length
	Average wait times (on peak days)		

World Bazaar

World Bazaar is the entrance to Tokyo Disneyland, taking you towards Cinderella Castle and beyond. This park entrance is similar in style to other parks' Main Street, U.S.A., and is themed to a small early-20th century American town. The first thing you will notice is that this area is all covered by a glass roof due to Tokyo's inclement weather.

World Bazaar contains many shops on both sides of the street, the king of which is the Grand Emporium, where you are sure to find something to buy!

There are restaurants along the street too, including Counter Service and Table Service restaurants, as well as snack locations. There are also other food shops and carts around World Bazaar too.

Main Street House is immediately to your left on Town Square; this is "Guest Services" and the equivalent of 'City Hall' in other parks. Ask any questions you have here. They can also make reservations for tours and restaurants, and accept complaints and positive feedback too.

Registration for the Disability Access Service and Separate Wait Service is available at Main Street House providing easier access to attractions. See our 'Guests with Disabilities' chapter for more information on this.

You will find character meets in this area of the park, as well as live music.

Silhouette Studio

Grab a unique souvenir here. Relax, as an artist cuts a silhouette from paper for a portrait of up to four people in one picture. Plus, you can even get Mickey or Minnie added in the picture with you. The whole process is done in just 2 to 3 minutes!

Portraits start at ¥920 for one person, ¥1,840 for two people, ¥2,750 for three people, and ¥3,670 for four people. A frame is an additional ¥1,080 to ¥1,300, depending on the one you choose. You can also add a stand for ¥200 to ¥800.

Penny Arcade

Step back in time into an old-fashioned style arcade that is suitable for the whole family. With pinball machines, fortune tellers, and claw games, this is the perfect place to stop over on a rainy day at the park.

Charges for games are not included in park admission, and each game costs between ¥100 and ¥300.

Omnibus

Ride Length: 5 to 7 minutes

The omnibus is a ride on an old-style double-decker bus around the Plaza in front of the castle. It allows you to get a glimpse of the other lands in the park.

Please note, unlike other Disney theme parks, where these vehicles travel up and down Main Street, the cars only go in the Plaza area in front of Cinderella Castle – you will be dropped off at the same point you board, so it is not a form of transportation.

Bibbidi Bobbidi Boutique

The Bibbidi Bobbidi Boutique is a makeover salon where little girls can be transformed into princesses complete with makeup, Disney dresses, and a hairdo. Then it's time for a photoshoot (optional)!

The Carriage Package is a 45-minute experience and includes makeup, a dress, and shoes. It is priced at ¥29,150 (approx. £205/€240/$260).

The Castle Package includes everything in the Carriage package, plus a photoshoot; this is a 75-minute experience costing ¥37,950 (approx. £265/€315/$350).

The Kingdom Package lasts 75 minutes and includes a studio photoshoot with the princess and her family. It costs ¥48,590 (approx. £345/€405/$450).

Finally, the Ultimate Castle Package with Photos lasts 1 hour 45 minutes and includes everything in the Kingdom Package, plus a photoshoot in the park; this is priced at ¥55,000 (approx. £385/€455/$505).

Reservations are required and can be made (in Japanese only) up to 1 month in advance using the link in the orange button at http://bit.ly/bibbiditokyo.

Dining:

Center Street Coffeehouse – Table Service location. Western cuisine. Breakfast set menus are ¥1,100 to ¥1,270 each. Lunch and dinner set meals are ¥1,500 to ¥1,980. A la carte desserts are ¥440. Drinks are ¥340 to ¥530. A children's set menu is ¥1,000, and a hypoallergenic menu is ¥1,100.

Eastside Café – Table Service location. Western Cuisine. Pasta meal with appetizer, pasta, bread and drink for ¥1,920. Dessert is an extra ¥500. The kids set menu is ¥1,100 and a hypoallergenic menu is ¥1,200.

Great American Waffle Co. – Snacks. A Mickey waffle is ¥500 to ¥750 depending on the toppings, drinks are ¥190 to ¥360.

Ice Cream Cones – Snack location. Ice creams are ¥300 to ¥500. Drinks are ¥300 to ¥360.

Refreshment Corner – Counter Service location. Hot dogs set menus are ¥840 to ¥890. A la carte hot dogs are ¥450 to ¥500, fries are ¥220, a cup salad is ¥360, and drinks are ¥190 to ¥360.

Restaurant Hokusai – Table Service location. Japanese cuisine. Set menus are between ¥1,880 to ¥2,280. A la carte desserts and drinks are ¥340 to ¥430. A children's set menu is ¥1,380, and the hypoallergenic menu is also ¥1,380.

Sweetheart Café – Snack location. Individual pastries are ¥200 to ¥370. A sandwich set is ¥990. Desserts are ¥200 to ¥460. Drinks are ¥190 to ¥360.

Adventureland

Tokyo Disneyland's Adventureland transports you to tropical jungles, the world of pirates, and other fun adventures. Most rides here are indoors or covered, making this an excellent place to head to when it is rainy and cold.

Pirates of the Caribbean

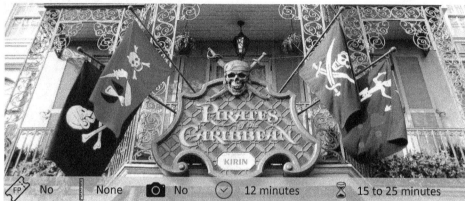

 No   None   No   12 minutes   15 to 25 minutes

On Pirates of the Caribbean guests board ships, which take them on a journey into a pirate world. There is a small flume drop, and there is a slight chance of a little splash or spray, but this is not a ride designed to get you wet.

The animatronic characters in the attraction are enthralling. Famous songs you will recognize are played throughout the attraction, adding to the Pirate-like atmosphere. You will even spot animatronics of Jack Sparrow.

The ride loads guests onto the boats efficiently, so the queue line is relatively fast-moving.

This is a definite must-see attraction while at Tokyo Disneyland and a true Disney classic.

Western River Railroad

No   None   No   15 minutes   10 to 20 minutes

This steam train takes you on a leisurely journey around (and through) Westernland, Critter Country, and Adventureland.

Unlike railroads at other Disney theme parks around the world, this one does not circle the entire park and only has one station where you board and then alight at the end of your trip.

Therefore, it is not a form of transportation, but it is still a great relaxing ride and gives you a unique viewpoint of many of the attractions in this area of the park.

You will also see parts of the park and details which are not accessible on foot.

Jungle Cruise: Wildlife Expeditions

FP No	None	No	9 minutes	15 to 25 minutes

Jump aboard and get ready to set sail through jungles across the world, seeing the world's animals with fun animatronics, and even some projection effects. On the boat, there is a skipper who is there to entertain you. Please note this ride is entirely in Japanese.

Although this ride takes place on the water, you won't get wet.

There is a special nighttime version of this attraction; it is worth seeing the ride both in the day and at night.

Swiss Family Treehouse

FP No	None	No	Walkthrough	None

Enter the world of Swiss Family Robinson as you explore the treehouse built from the wood of their shipwreck. You can see the complex water wheel system they built to get water up to the bedrooms, explore the kitchen, living rooms, and bedrooms.

This is a walkthrough experience, and kids are generally fans of exploring and climbing the steps. There are panels throughout the walk in each section with explanations in both English and Japanese.

From the top, the view is mostly obscured by the leaves, but you can get an interesting perspective on the park from up here with great views of Cinderella Castle.

The Enchanted Tiki Room: Stitch Presents "Aloha E Komo Mai!"

This is perhaps one of the most bizarre attractions in the park – a 10-minute show where birds, flowers, and Stitch (of 'Lilo and Stitch' fame) sing together. You can also expect to see the Tiki Gods.

The show is entirely in Japanese with the option for English subtitles available via a handheld device – simply ask a Cast Member for this when joining the queue.

FP | No | None | ✓ 10 minutes | ⧖ Until next show

Theatre Orleans

This is a small outdoor theater and shows change regularly. Shows are generally Latin-themed, with classic Disney characters and catchy songs.

This theater uses the ticket lottery system to guarantee a seat (see the 'Show Lotteries' section of the 'Understanding the Parks' chapter) for a detailed guide on how this works. For unfilled seats, a standby queue may be used. Unlike other venues, you can also stand outside the main seating area and watch the show from here.

Dining

Blue Bayou Restaurant – Table service location inside 'Pirates of the Caribbean' ride. Western cuisine. The Blue Bayou set meal is ¥4,500 to ¥5,200. The children's set menu is ¥1,800, and a low allergen menu is ¥1,900.

Boiler Room Bites – Snack location. Snacks and drinks priced between ¥190 and ¥600.

Café Orléans – Snack location. Sells crepes for ¥450. Drinks are ¥300 to ¥360.

China Voyager – Counter Service location. Chinese cuisine. Noodle soups are priced at ¥1030 to ¥1200 each. Set menus with a drink, and a bun as a side is ¥1,480 to ¥1,650. Sides such as buns, pork rice, and eggs are ¥100 to ¥460 each. Drinks and desserts are also available. The children's set menu is ¥780.

Crystal Palace Restaurant – Buffet restaurant. Western and Japanese cuisines. The adult price is ¥3,150, children aged 7 to 12 years pay ¥2,000, and children aged 4 to 6 years are ¥1,250. Free refills of soft drinks and hot drinks are included. The breakfast here is a set menu – pricing is ¥1,850 per adult, and ¥1,230 per child. There is a 90-minute time limit. This is a great option for big eaters.

Fresh Fruit Oasis – Snack location. Fresh fruit cups are ¥450 each. This location also sells teas and fruit juices at around ¥200 each.

Parkside Wagon – Snack location. Churros are priced at ¥350 to ¥400 each.

Polynesian Terrace Restaurant – Table Service restaurant with Disney characters and 1-hour show. Western cuisine. Lunch is priced between ¥3,770 and ¥4,610 for adults with kids' seats (ages 4 to 8) priced at ¥2,730 to ¥3,570. The dinner show is ¥4,190 to ¥5,030 for adults, and kids meals are ¥2,830 to ¥3,670. Advanced online reservations are required for this dinner show (in Japanese only) – maximum one month in advance.

Royal Street Veranda – Snack location. Sells mini cakes and drinks at ¥300 to ¥850.

Squeezer's Tropical Juice Bar – Drinks location. Drinks are priced between ¥300 and ¥450. Also offers soft-serve ice cream seasonally.

The Gazebo – Snack location. Wraps are ¥500. Soft drinks & hot drinks are ¥300 to ¥360.

The Skipper's Galley – Snack location. Teriyaki chicken legs are ¥500 each.

Westernland

Westernland is the equivalent of the Wild West-themed Frontierland in the American Disney parks. However, the word 'Frontier' does not translate well into Japanese, so here they have dubbed this area Westernland.

Big Thunder Mountain

| FP Yes | 102cm | 📷 No | ✓ 3 minute 30 seconds | ⏳ 90 to 120 minutes |

Jump aboard a family rollercoaster sure to bring a smile to everyone's face. This ride lasts about three and a half minutes, which is unusually long for a rollercoaster.

You will see explosives, western towns, flooding caves, bats, and more on this wild, wild ride! This is a great family ride and a way to get kids into rollercoasters, being the first real rollercoaster for many.

We have heard rumblings that a Single Rider queue line may be making an appearance in 2020, so be sure to ask a Cast Member at the attraction entrance to see if this has been implemented in time for your visit.

Tom Sawyer Island Rafts

 No | None | No | Free exploration | Less than 5 minutes

Take a raft over to Tom Sawyer's Island and explore this well-themed area with a treehouse, caves, buried treasure, floating bridges, a fort, an Indian camp, and much more. You can easily spend a good 20 minutes, just wandering around this area.

Westernland Shootin' Gallery

This is a shooting gallery as is seen at many fairgrounds; here, it is themed to the Wild West. When you hit a target, it triggers a reaction.

There is an extra charge (¥200) to use this attraction as it is not included in regular park admission.

Main Twain Riverboat

Sail on the Rivers of America on a leisurely cruise as you enjoy the sights.

This attraction begins operating one hour after Park opening.

Closing times may vary seasonally – please check with a Cast Member.

 No | None | ✓ 12 minutes | ⧗ Less than 20 minutes

Woodchuck Greeting Trail

This character meeting opportunity allows you to meet Disney characters wearing explorer or scout outfits. Usually, the characters here are Donald and Daisy.

Country Bear Theater

 No | None | 📷 No | ✓ 16 minutes | ⧗ Until next show

The Country Bear Jamboree is a sit-down theatre-show style attraction with pre-recorded singing from a series of animatronic bears.

To be honest, it is probably our least favorite attraction in the park as it is very outdated and has never

resonated with us. On the other hand, it does provide shelter from the rain and heat and allows for a sit-down break with no queue lines.

Go in if you have the time, but do not make it a priority and do not expect any

miracles from the show. The show is almost entirely in Japanese, including all the dialogue (bizarrely some songs are in English).

There are three versions of the show: a regular version, a Christmas version, and a summer version.

Dining

Camp Woodchuck Kitchen – Counter Service location. Hamburgers/sandwiches are ¥710 to ¥1,100 as a meal. A vegetarian set meal and drink is ¥1,200. Also serves smoked turkey legs for ¥800. Sides, snacks and drinks are ¥140 to ¥500.

Cowboy Cookhouse – Snack location. Serves smoked turkey legs for ¥800 each.

Hungry Bear Restaurant – Counter Service location. Curry dishes are ¥800 to ¥1,300. A kids' menu is ¥620, and a low allergen menu is ¥820. Sides, desserts and drinks are also sold.

Pecos Bill Café – Snack location. Serves pork rice rolls for ¥500 and churros for ¥350. Also serves hot drinks and soft drinks for ¥300 to ¥360.

Plaza Pavilion Restaurant – Counter Service location (Buffeteria Style). Western cuisine. Main courses are priced at ¥1150; sides cost between ¥220 and ¥530, desserts range from ¥370 to ¥420. The children's set menu is ¥940. A low allergen meal is ¥1,040.

The Diamond Horseshoe – Table Service location with a live show (entertainment lasts 1 hour). Western cuisine. Lunch is ¥3,350 to ¥4,190 for adults depending on seats chosen, for kids (ages 4 to 8) it is ¥2,300 to ¥3,150. Dinner is ¥4,190 to ¥5,030 for adults, and ¥2,830 to ¥3,670 for kids (ages 4 to 8). Advanced online reservations are required and can be made up to 1 month in advance.

Critter Country

Located on the banks of the Rivers of America, here tales from the American South come to life.

Splash Mountain

Yes	90cm	Yes	10 minutes	90 to 150 minutes

Hop on a ride inspired by Br'er Rabbit's adventure and the 'Song of the South' film.

This is a log flume-style ride with a long indoor portion and includes scenes following the story of the movie.

Enjoy the great music, the animatronics and the details, the small indoor drops, as well as the big 52-foot drop at the end.

You can get soaked on this ride – unlike its Walt Disney World counterpart, which merely sprays its guests.

A Single Rider queue line is available – we have found this to be a huge timesaver as Fastpasses for this ride regularly run out quickly.

Beaver Brothers Explorer Canoes

No	See below	No	10 to 20 minutes	15 to 30 minutes

This is yet another way to get around the Rivers of America. This time, you provide the power as you use real oars to paddle in a canoe to sail around the island.

As groups of twenty power at the same time, it is less effort than it might appear – an interesting and unique theme park experience. Cast Members will do their speech in Japanese but will also repeat important safety information in English.

This attraction may not operate during non-peak days. This attraction closes at dusk. Guests under age seven must wear a life jacket. Guests whose feet cannot reach the floor when seated may not ride.

Dining

Grandma Sara's Kitchen – Counter Service. Western cuisine. Mains are priced at ¥1120 to ¥1320, and between ¥1340 and ¥1540 with a drink. Sides, desserts, and drinks are also available. The kid's menu is priced at ¥940, and a low allergen menu is ¥1040.
Rackety's Racoon Saloon – Snack location. Serves tortilla dogs (¥350 to ¥400), churros for ¥350, ice creams for ¥300 to ¥450, and drinks.

Fantasyland

Fantasyland is the place to entertain the younger members of the family with attractions based around Disney classics.

Pooh's Hunny Hunt

 Yes | None | No | 4 minutes | 90 to 120 minutes

Enter one of Winnie the Pooh's "hunny" pots and explore this magnificent world as created by A. A. Milne. Once seated, you will ride from scene to scene, meeting Tigger, Pooh, and their friends.

The ride uses a trackless technology, so each ride vehicle takes a different route on each ride, making for some very different experiences each time.

This ride gets one of the lengthiest waits in the park and is a fun, family-friendly adventure. It should be a priority for obtaining a Fastpass or riding at the start of the day.

Cinderella's Fairy Tale Hall

No | None | No | Walkthrough | 20 to 30 minutes

Cinderella's Fairy Tale Hall is a walkthrough attraction inside Cinderella Castle. As you move from room to room, you can see pictures and sculptures retelling the Cinderella story.

Along the way, there are

many great photo opportunities such as a throne to sit on, and you can try and see if your feet are the right size to find in Cinderella's glass slipper.

This is not a meet-and-greet with the princesses.

This attraction is closed until early April 2020 for refurbishment.

Fun Fact: Take photos with the flash on. In your photos, you will see extra details that are not visible to the naked eye.

Alice's Tea Party

 No | None | No | 1 minute 30 seconds | Less than 20 minutes

Hop inside one of the teacups from Alice in Wonderland and start spinning wildly.

The ride functions much like any other teacup ride around the world; you have a wheel at the center of the

cup, and you can turn it to spin yourself around faster, or leave it alone and have a more relaxing spin.

Cinderella Castle

Step inside Cinderella's castle and walk under the main entranceway across the moat and into Fantasyland.

Standing at 168 feet tall, the castle is the central icon of the Tokyo Disneyland and indeed the whole of Tokyo Disney Resort.

Like some of the other Disney castles such as those at the Disneyland Resort and Disneyland Paris, you can go inside the castle in the attraction 'Cinderella's Fairy Tale Hall' listed earlier.

Cinderella is undergoing a significant refurbishment until April 2020, so it may have scaffolding on its facades during your visit. The area around and inside the castle will also be subject to closures.

Mickey's Philharmagic

Philharmagic is a fun 4D show, and in our opinion, one that should not be missed.

The story is that you are attending Goofy's opera performance with Mickey's Philharmonic orchestra. When Donald gets involved, however, things get a little out of hand, and you end up on an adventure traveling through a world of Disney classics. Do not miss this fun show with short waits!

With an air-conditioned queue line and theater, shelter from the rain, and a fantastic musical movie, it is easy to see why this attraction has one of the highest guest satisfaction ratings in the whole of the

No | None | 15 minutes | 5 to 10 minutes

Magic Kingdom.

The audio for this show, including all dialogue and songs, is in Japanese – you won't have any trouble following the storyline, though, as it is essentially a mash-up of Disney's greatest hit songs.

Top Tip: At the show's conclusion, when Donald flies off the screen, and the curtain goes down, look at the back of the theater for an extra special surprise.

Peter Pan's Flight

| FP No | None | No | 3 minutes | 30 to 45 minutes |

Board a flying pirate ship and take a voyage through the world of Peter Pan and Never Never Land. The scenes will be both beside you and (because you are in a flying pirate ship) below you too!

The interior to this ride is stunning from the moment you step in, and the whole experience is truly immersive.

If you are afraid of heights, this ride may not be suitable for you as the ships give the sensation of flight, and at times you will be several feet off the ground.

Snow White's Adventures

| FP No | None | No | 2 minutes 30 seconds | 20 to 30 minutes |

Step inside the world of Snow White as you venture through the major scenes in the movie on a classic dark ride.

Although the ride is, for the most part, tame, several moments may frighten younger children – these make up a significant portion of the ride. In other Disney Parks, this ride is actually known as Snow White's *Scary* Adventures.

Nevertheless, this is an enjoyable retelling of Walt Disney's first feature film.

Haunted Mansion

| FP Yes | None | 📷 No | ✓ 7 minutes | ⧗ 45 to 90 minutes |

This ride is sure to get the whole family spooked, as you venture through the derelict haunted mansion. The attraction is part-walkthrough and part-ride. Guests ride in "doombuggies" which rotate and tilt to show scenes around them.

It is in no way a horror-maze type attraction, and you will find that almost everyone loves the ride – it is fun and not scary.

Most of the Disney parks

around the world have a slightly altered version of this ride, and it is a true Disney classic.

Beware that the mansion may frighten some younger children. There are not any jump-out scares, but the loud laughter during the initial walkthrough section may be frightening, as well as the pop-up ghosts when you reach the cemetery scenes of the ride itself.

During the Halloween and Holiday seasons, the entire

decor is re-themed to Tim Burton's 'A Nightmare Before Christmas' – this makes the attraction a completely different experience; during this time, this almost is a different ride altogether.

If you go before or after these seasons, be aware the attraction may be closed for its transition period. The waits for this ride during the Holiday overlay are typically longer than the rest of the year.

Mickey's Philharmagic

Ride through the story of Pinocchio, and see the tales from the movie turn to life in front of your very eyes.

There are a few clever effects inside the ride and, as with the movie, there are also some darker moments that may frighten younger children, though these do pass by relatively quickly and are generally fine for most children.

| FP No | None | ✓ 2 minutes | ⧗ 10 to 20 minutes |

Dumbo The Flying Elephant

Step aboard and fly through the skies with Dumbo! Situated right in the center of Fantasyland, it offers views of the surrounding area, as well as being a whole lot of fun. In front of the Dumbo elephant seats, there is a lever to lift your Dumbo up or down!

Due to its popularity, its slow loading nature and low hourly capacity, Dumbo has reasonably long queues all day long - try to ride it during parades, or the beginning or end of the day

| FP | No | None | 1 minute 30 seconds | 30 to 45 minutes |

for the shortest waits. This is one of the most popular rides in Fantasyland.

"it's a small world"

One of the most memorable and popular park attractions, "it's a small world" features hundreds of dolls singing along to a catchy tune about the uniting of the world.

As your boat sails leisurely through the attraction, you can enjoy sights and sounds from around the world.

The loading system is efficient, meaning that the number of people who can enjoy the ride every hour is high; this means wait times are usually low, and there is a continually moving queue line.

| FP | No | None | 14 minutes | 15 to 30 minutes |

This is a great Disney classic that, although not based on any film franchise, is a "must-do" for most visitors.

Top Tip: Look out for the dolls designed to look like Disney characters on the ride. You will see everyone from Stitch to Woody.

Fantasyland Forest Theatre (Opens 15th April 2020)

This new theater will open with the expansion of Fantasyland on 15th April 2020. This will be Tokyo Disneyland's first indoor theater and will be designed to look like it is located in a forest.

The theater will open with a unique new show 'Mickey's

Magical Music World' in which Mickey and his pals find a music box deep in the forest. A magical journey follows with scenes and characters from Beauty and the Beast, Jungle Book, The Little Mermaid, Peter Pan, and much more.

The show will last about 25 minutes, with 5 to 9 performances per day, depending on the season. At the moment, we do not know if this attraction will use the ticket lottery system like the other shows in the park or if it will be a standby or Fastpass show.

Enchanted Tale of Beauty and the Beast (Opens 15th April 2020)

| FP Yes | None | No | 8 minutes | 120 to 180 minutes (estimated) |

The newest major attraction at the Tokyo Disney Resort will open in 2020. This Beauty and the Beast-themed ride will take you aboard an enchanted teacup and spinning through scenes from the timeless movie. You will enter the Beast's castle to board, dance in a banquet with Lumiere and other classic characters, and even see Belle and the Beast dancing in the snow.

Until the ride opens, we can only use the information that has been released to guide you.

The announced ride length of 8 minutes will likely include a pre-show as a ride of this length is almost unheard of. The actual ride will probably last 4 to 6 minutes. We anticipate this to be the most popular attraction at the resort for the next couple of years and expect wait times to remain above two hours for all of 2020 daily.

The ride will feature both Fastpass and Single Rider, and with teacups seating ten guests, we can see the Single Rider being extremely valuable here. The attraction will be part of Happy15 early entry for hotel guests, so we would recommend going here first if you have access to Happy15. Otherwise, a Fastpass for this should be your top priority.

Dining

Captain Hook's Galley – Counter Service location. Pizza slices are ¥500 to ¥550, and set menus with a drink are also available for ¥720 to ¥820. Also sells side dishes such as baked cheese potatoes, and drinks.

Cleo's – Snack location. Cakes and drinks are priced around ¥350 each.

La Taverne de Gaston (Opens 15 April 2020) – Counter Service location. Serves 'big bite croissants', French toast sandwiches and Hunter's Pie. Each is ¥750 as an individual item or ¥1,140 as a set meal.

LeFou's (Opens 15 April 2020) – Snack location. Serves apple-caramel churros for ¥400, and other snacks.

Magical Market – Snack location. Serves seasonal food. The menu changed regularly.

Queen of Hearts Banquet Hall – Counter Service location (Buffeteria-style). Western cuisine. Main courses are priced between ¥1300 and ¥1580. Side dishes are ¥400 to ¥720. Desserts (including an unbirthday cake) and drinks are also available.

Troubadour Tavern – Snack location. Ice creams are ¥300 to ¥500. Drinks cost ¥300 to ¥360.

Village Pastry – Snack location. Snacks are around ¥350 each.

Toontown

Visit the fun town where Mickey and his pals live and play.

Roger Rabbit's Car Toon Spin

Step into the world of Roger Rabbit in this ride with a twist!

In your car, you can choose to sit back and enjoy the storyline or turn the wheel in the center of your taxi to spin round as you go through the scenes. It is a surprisingly surreal experience to have this level of control on a dark ride, and it makes every ride different from the last.

 No | None | 3 minutes | 25 to 45 minutes

Gadget's Go Coaster

 No | 90cm | No | 1 minute | 15 to 30 minutes

A small rollercoaster for kids with one drop and a few turns – adult and thrill-seekers will likely find the ride rather underwhelming. However, this is not made for adults - it is a good starter coaster for kids before getting them on the likes of Big Thunder Mountain.

Minnie's House

Step inside Minnie Mouse's house. This is a short walkthrough experience with a variety of different interactive elements – for example, when you touch the oven or the dishwasher something very magical may happen. Note that this is not a permanent meet and greet location with Minnie.

Mickey's House and Meet Mickey

This attraction is similar to Minnie's House, but for the big cheese himself. Even better once you have made your way through the house and entered his movie studio, you get to *meet* Mickey! A Disney photographer is present, and you will have the opportunity to take photos, including with your own camera.

This often has one of the longest waits in the park.

No | None | Yes | 45 to 90 minutes

Chip 'n Dale's Treehouse

This is another of this area's walkthrough attractions.

You can climb the steps up the treehouse and see how the two cheeky chipmunks have made this place home.

Please note that this is not a character meet and greet location.

Donald's Boat

You will no doubt see the imposing boat on Toon Lake – this a walkthrough of Donald Duck's boat, the Miss Daisy. Climb the decks and play with the various interactive elements. This is not a character meet and greet location.

Goofy's Paint 'n' Play House

This is a cool little side attraction where every few minutes a small group of guests can enter Goofy's Play House and help him redecorate.

With the help of projections, screens, and eight 'Splat Master' guns, you can point your gun at the walls and furniture and help splat the room with paint. The experience lasts about 1 minute 30 seconds.

Minnie's Style Studio (Opens 15th April 2020)

This new attraction will be a counterpart to 'Meet Mickey,' where here you will be able to find a permanent meet-and-greet location for Minnie Mouse.

As a world-renowned fashion designer, Minnie Mouse will greet guests while wearing her latest design, which will change each season. Minnie's Style Studio is where she designs, creates, and photographs her new fashions. Guests enter the lobby where posters of magazine covers featuring Minnie are on display, visit her office where she draws her original designs, and then pass through the workroom where Minnie's designs become outfits.

Finally, guests will enter the photo studio where Minnie will greet them wearing her latest high-fashion design for the season. Minnie's costumes will come in four designs, one to match each season.

We expect waits to be similar to Meet Mickey and average around 45 to 90 minutes.

Dining

Dinghy Drinks – Drinks location. Drinks are priced between ¥240 and ¥800.
Huey, Dewey and Louie's Good Time Café – Counter Service location. Individual pizza and burger items are ¥560 to ¥600. A meal with a drink and fries is ¥950 to ¥990. Snacks, drinks, side items and desserts are also available.
Mickey's Trailer – Snack location. Sells large spring rolls for ¥350.
Pop-A-Lot Popcorn – Snack location. Sells popcorn priced at ¥400 or with a souvenir bucket for an extra charge.
Toon Pop – Snack location. Sells popcorn (¥400) or with a souvenir bucket for extra.
Toontone Treats – Snack location. Sells long nan with meat sauce for ¥500, and drinks.

Tomorrowland

Adventure into a world far away in this land from the future.

Pooh's Hunny Hunt

| FP Yes | None | 📷 Yes | ✓ 5 minutes | ⏳ 90 to 120 minutes |

Explore the world of Monsters, Inc. as you board a security vehicle armed with flashlights. As you move in your car, familiar scenes will play out - point your flashlight at the Monsters Inc. logos, and special effects will trigger. This is a fun, family-friendly ride, and fans of the film franchise are sure to enjoy seeing their favorite characters here.

Buzz Lightyear Astro Blasters

This ride is great family-fun as you step aboard the Space Cruisers and use the onboard laser guns to shoot at targets around you – you will be helping out Buzz Lightyear, and racking up points as you shoot the different targets.

Different targets are worth different amounts of points, and there are even hidden targets that allow you to score thousands of points in one go.

You can even affect the direction of your Space Cruiser with a joystick in the middle and turn the car the other way if you spot a target your friend has not.

| FP Yes | None | ✓ 5 minutes | ⏳ 60 to 90 minutes |

If you have been to Walt Disney World, this is similar to the ride in Magic Kingdom Park but with different scenes and with detachable guns for even more fun!

At the end of the ride, the person with the most points wins. It is competitive and endlessly re-rideable. Great fun.

Star Tours

FP	Yes	102cm	📷 No	⌄ 4 minutes 30 seconds	⏳ 45 to 90 minutes

From the moment you step into the queue line, you are transported into an intergalactic spaceport with adverts for various destinations and overhead announcements of flights leaving.

As you travel through the Space terminal, you will see StarSpeeders, an alien Air Traffic Control station, R2-D2, C3PO, and many robots hard at work to make your journey into space

unforgettable.

Staff will split you into groups, and then you board your vehicle for your tour to one of many planets. Each ride is an unforgettable adventure, and each time you experience the ride, it should be slightly different, with over 50 different combinations of scenes picked randomly!

However, if you are prone to motion sickness or are not

comfortable with confined spaces, Star Tours will most probably not be for you. If you want a milder ride, ask to be sat on the front row as this is the middle of the vehicle, and therefore there are fewer sudden movements.

The Fastpass distribution machines for this ride are not located next to the ride, but next to Tomorrowland Hall near Space Mountain.

Stitch Encounter

Enter a special transmission room, and a Cast Member will connect your party with Stitch. You will be speaking with him live in space. Stitch is curious about how the planet Earth works, so he will ask all sorts of questions to learn about our home.

All in all, this attraction is good fun, but foreign guests will likely have difficulty with this show as it is presented entirely in Japanese.

FP	No	None	⌄ 12 minutes	⏳ Less than 15 minutes

Space Mountain

| FP Yes | 102cm | No | 2 minutes 30 seconds | 90 to 150 minutes |

Space Mountain is a rollercoaster through space designed with the family in mind - it has no loops or inversions and recreates the feeling of soaring through the galactic world.

We strongly recommend a Fastpass as the queue line is not themed at all and ends up feeling even longer than it is. Alternatively, get to this ride first or last to minimize wait times.

Note that this ride is tamer than its Walt Disney World counterpart, and much tamer than the Disneyland Paris version. It is almost an exact clone of the Disneyland Resort version of the ride.

The Happy Ride with Baymax (Opens 15th April 2020)

The brilliant young inventor Hiro Hamada from the Big Hero 6 movie learned from his robotic personal healthcare companion Baymax that the first step in making people healthy is to make them happy, so he and Baymax developed this wild, musical ride that is sure to make everyone happy.

As Hiro's favorite up-tempo music plays, guests aboard vehicles pulled by Baymax's nursebot friends can enjoy being whirled around in unexpected ways. A device on the attraction's ceiling

| FP Yes | 81cm | 1 minute 30 seconds | 45 to 90 minutes |

"scans" the guests with lights to measure their happiness while on the ride. The levels of happiness are

sure to be high as guests enjoy the surprises and unexpected twists of the ride.

Showbase (Tomorrowland Shows)

Showbase housed the park's most popular daytime stage show, One Man's Dream. However, a temporary show will replace this from 10th January to 19th March 2020 called It's Very Minnie.

The show which will replace 'It's Very Minnie' from March onwards had not been announced at the time of writing.

The information below is valid for all shows presented at Showbase.

The first show of the day is first come-first seated. Subsequent shows have some unreserved seats but most seated are filled with a lottery ticket system. You will need to visit Tomorrowland Hall to attempt the lottery (to the left of Space Mountain).

Once inside, go to the touchscreen machine, follow the on-screen instructions (an English option is available): choose a show time, scan all your party's tickets, and then press the next button. If you win, a ticket will be printed out with your reserved seat number and performance time.

You may only attempt the lottery once per day per show and must have all tickets present for each member of your party who wishes to view the show.

Dining

Pan Galactic Pizza Port – Counter Service. Sells pizzas and calzones for ¥620 to ¥740 each and meal options are priced between ¥840 and ¥960. Salads, desserts and drinks are also available. Serves the Green Alien mochi dumplings.

Plaza Ray's Diner – Counter Service. Sells Asian style take-away meals at ¥800 or ¥1190 with a side and a drink.

Soft Landing – Snack location. Sells ice creams and drinks. Ice cream cones or cups are ¥300 to ¥360 each. Located along the upper exit walkway of Star Tours.

The Popping Pod – Snack location. Sells popcorn boxes for ¥400.

Tomorrowland Terrace – Counter Service. Sells burgers for ¥600 and a meal for ¥990. Nuggets, desserts and drinks are also available.

Tokyo Disneyland Park Entertainment

Dreaming Up! – Daytime Parade

See almost every Disney character you could want in this exciting parade. For many guests, this is the highlight of their day. You can expect to see many huge and amazingly beautiful floats with your favorite Disney characters on board, as well as dancers and much more.

During the 18-minute parade, you usually can expect to see the following characters: Mickey, Minnie, Pluto, Goofy, Cheshire Cat, Tweedle Dum and Tweedle Dee, Alice, The Mad Hatter, The King and Queen of Hearts, Jiminy Cricket, Pinocchio, Geppetto, The Fairy Godmother, Rapunzel, Snow White, Cinderella, Aurora, Chip 'n Dale, Belle, Winnie the Pooh, Piglet, Tigger, Donald and Daisy Duck, Hiro Hamada (from 'Big Hero 6'), Mary Poppins and Bert, Peter Pan and Wendy, the Three Little Pigs, the Big Bad Wolf, Clarabelle Cow, and Horace Horseshoe, Max, Scrooge McDuck, Perla and Suzy (Cinderella's mice), Aladdin and Jasmine.

The atmosphere, the amazing soundtrack, and all the enthusiasm are sure to make the parade one of the highlights of your visit.

The parades are very busy with a large number of guests, but guests are generally very well-behaved, and the first few rows of guests sit on the ground allowing those behind them to still get a better view. Guests will start staking out spots over an hour in advance, but if you are happy to stand (and be a few rows back), you can usually turn up just 15 minutes before or even later.

The parade route is entirely different to the other Disney Magic Kingdom-style theme parks, mainly because this park does not have a "Main Street" at its entrance. Here the parade begins in Fantasyland to the right of Haunted Mansion; it then briefly enters Westernland going past The Diamond Horseshoe, circles the hub in front of the castle, enters Tomorrowland going past the left side of Tomorrowland Terrace concluding in Toontown by the food area.

A seasonal parade may be performed in addition to this daily parade at certain times of the year, such as Easter.

Jamboree Mickey – Interactive Daytime Show

This new dance program debuted in October 2019, and takes place in front of Cinderella Castle. It invites younger Guests (ages 11 and under) to learn some new moves with Mickey and Friends. Participating children can have fun dancing around with the Disney Pals to music based on the well-loved "Mickey Mouse March."

Jamboree Mickey lasts about 15 minutes.

Disney Light the Night – Nighttime Show – Fireworks

This is the park's nightly fireworks display with pyrotechnics timed to famous Disney tunes.; this is an 'old-style' nighttime show featuring just fireworks and no projections on the castle.

It is a very short 5-minute spectacle, and views are good from anywhere in the park, and the fireworks can even be seen from Tokyo DisneySea. The fireworks do not frame the castle in any way, so there is no need to stake out a specific spot in advance.

Be aware that due to high winds in the area, this show may be canceled. You should see 'Disney Light the Night' as a bonus show in addition to the nighttime parade, and not as the must-see event of the evening.

Dreaming Up! – Daytime Parade

This stunning, 20-minute-long nighttime parade takes the same route as the daytime "Dream Up!" parade, starting in Fantasyland and ending in Toontown. Here all your favorite characters parade by with their costumes and floats covered in thousands of sparkling lights.

Fans of Disney's Main Street Electrical Parade, which has been performed around the world, will be pleased to hear the same catchy soundtrack used for part of the soundtrack and may also recognize a few floats. However, most of the parade is unique to Tokyo Disneyland.

During the parade you can expect to see huge floats and characters from the following movies: Alice in Wonderland, Snow White, Pete's Dragon, Peter Pan, Finding Nemo, Toy Story, Aladdin, Tangled, Cinderella, Beauty and the Beast, Frozen, as well as many other characters. The parade is presented in a mixture of English and Japanese – this does not negatively affect its enjoyment at all.

If the parade cannot be presented due to rain, a unique alternative parade is performed instead called "Nightfall Glow" – this parade runs the route backward starting in Toontown and ending in Fantasyland.

Tokyo DisneySea

Tokyo DisneySea is the second theme park at the Tokyo Disney Resort. It is composed of seven original themed lands (or 'Ports of Call' as they are called here): Mediterranean Harbor, American Waterfront, Port Discovery, Lost River Delta, Arabian Coast, Mermaid Lagoon, and Mysterious Island. The park is centered around Mount Prometheus, a Disney-created volcano which occasionally erupts with flames coming out of the top.

Unlike Tokyo Disneyland Park, which is based on the original Disneyland, the Imagineers went in a whole new direction with this theme park. Disney Parks enthusiasts will recognize a few of the attractions in this theme park, but each is presented uniquely – plus, they are sure to find many adventures which cannot be found in any other Disney park.

Tokyo DisneySea is the second most visited theme park outside of the USA, and the fourth most-visited in the world, with 14.7 million visitors in 2018. It is just behind Tokyo Disneyland in terms of visitor numbers.

Expect to wait longer for the major rides at this park than at Tokyo Disneyland as it has fewer attractions and contains many big 'headliner' rides. However, when walking around, this park feels less crowded as this park is about 50% larger than Tokyo Disneyland.

We will now take a look at each port individually, as well as their attractions, dining options, and other notable features.

Waiting in queue lines is inevitable at theme parks. To help you determine how long you may wait to experience the attractions, we have included "average wait times"; these are for peak times such as school holidays (Summer, Christmas, Golden Week) and weekends throughout the year. Wait times outside busy times are often lower.

Important Note: The park's iconic volcano, Mount Prometheus, will be undergoing refurbishment until sometime in October 2020, meaning it may be fully or partially covered in scaffolding during your visit.

Mediterranean Harbor

Mediterranean Harbor is the entrance 'port of call' of Tokyo DisneySea. Here you will find an abundance of shopping and dining options, as well as one of the park's most popular attractions.

Mediterranean Harbor is the entrance 'port of call' of Tokyo DisneySea. Here you will find an abundance of shopping and dining options, as well as one of the park's most popular attractions.

Mediterranean Harbor is the equivalent of World Bazaar in Tokyo Disneyland.

This theming of this area of the park is simply beautiful and designed to resemble a Southern European (Italian) port town.

The buildings by the entrance and looking over the lagoon are not merely facades, but actually the rooms and public areas of the 5-star MiraCosta Hotel.

This is also where you will find many park services, including Guest Relations, Storage Lockers, Lost Children, and First Aid.

Soaring: Fantastic Flight

FP Yes	102cm	📷 No	⌄ 5 minutes	⏳ 120 to 180 minutes

This is the park's most popular attraction at the moment, as it is the newest having opened in July 2019. On extremely busy days, we have seen the waits for this ride get up to 320 minutes.

At the time of writing, the attraction has been closing its standby queue a couple of hours before park closing and only allowing those with Fastpass reservations to access the ride; this may well continue throughout 2020, so do not count on this being open at the end of the day.

Soaring: Fantastic Flight gives you the chance to experience what it is like to fly over iconic locations from around the world. It is largely the same experience as in the American Disney parks, but with a different preshow and theming.

It is a truly immersive experience with smells and slow movement to match a giant on-screen video, creating an incredibly realistic sensation of flight. If you are scared of heights, this ride is most definitely not for you.

For us, the attraction does not warrant the huge waits it is getting at the moment, even though the concept is simple, and the execution is excellent. We recommend making this your first stop as soon as the park opens for a Fastpass.

Fortress Explorations

This walkthrough area is a chance to get some learning during your visit – as you explore the galleon and fortress, you can learn from various exhibitions on offer about planets, nautical instruments, and much more. The fort is home to the fictional Society of Explorers and Adventurers (S.E.A. – as in DisneySEA).

This is perhaps the best-themed walkthrough attraction ever created, and has an intricate storyline. There are plaques in many rooms explaining what you

 No None Walkthrough None

are looking at, but to appreciate the interactivity in this area, we recommend

taking the free Leonardo Challenge – see the next listing.

Leonardo Challenge

Located inside Fortress Explorations, the Leonardo Challenge is an interactive adventure where you follow hints and clues on a map (provided by Cast Members) to become a member of an exclusive explorer troupe. This challenge starts 1 or 2 hours after park opening (or

sometimes at midday) and ends at sunset – consult a Cast Member in the area of Guest Relations. There are a limited number of maps each day.

There are several different colored trails, and each has its own unique puzzles.

Unfortunately, the map is available in Japanese only – you could try using a translation app such as Google Translate to do this. Alternatively, Youtuber 'DaydreamerVlogs' has made a video for each map explaining what you need to do for these challenges.

DisneySea Transit Steamer Line

 No None No 5 to 10 minutes Less than 15 minutes

Get around Tokyo DisneySea in style aboard a steamer boat.

There are stops at Mediterranean Harbor, American Waterfront, and Lost River Delta.

Get a unique perspective on this beautiful park as you

sail around and see corners of the park only visible from the steamers.

Please note that operation is stopped during preparations for shows on the harbor, and resumes after the performance.

Venetian Gondolas

FP No	None	📷 No	⌄ 10 minutes	⏳ 15 to 30 minutes

Enjoy a relaxing ride around the Palazzo Canals as your gondolier shows you the sights (and they may even sing!). This is the real deal with the gondoliers actually paddling (there is no hidden ride system doing all the heavy work). Please note that the gondola is not private, and you will share it with other people – each seats 16 people. The gondoliers will speak only in Japanese, but you are here for the views anyway!

The operation is stopped during the preparations for shows on the harbor and resumes after the performance ends. This means that there are frequent interruptions to the service of this attraction.

Dining

Cafe Portofino – Counter Service. Mains are priced between ¥1280 and ¥2500 with options including rotisserie chicken, and seafood linguine. Sides, desserts and drinks are also available. A 2-course set meal is available for ¥1920 including a drink.

Gondolier Snacks – Snack location. Ice creams in warmer weather are priced around ¥400. In colder weather, wraps and sandwiches are sold at ¥500 to ¥600.

Magellan's – Table Service. Western menu. Two lunch set menus are available priced at ¥3700 and ¥4600 for three courses with no drinks. Two dinner set menus are available priced at ¥5800 and ¥8000. The kids set menu is ¥2100; the low allergen menu is ¥2200.

Magellan's Lounge – Drinks lounge. As well as a wide selection on alcoholic and non-alcoholic drinks, appetizers and desserts are available and priced between ¥470 and ¥1480.

Mamma Biscotti's Bakery – Snack location. Serves bakery items for ¥200 to ¥420. Other snacks and drinks are also available. Sells the Green Alien mochi dumplings.

Refrescos – Snack location. Serves smoked turkey legs (¥800), soft drinks and beer (¥620).

Ristorante di Canaletto – Table Service. Western cuisine. A three-course set menu with a drink is ¥2900. A la carte mains are ¥1720 to ¥1920. The kids' menu is priced at ¥1500 and a low allergen menu is ¥1600. Vegetarian options are available.

Zambini Brothers' Ristorante – Counter Service. Serves pizzas priced at ¥880, and pasta dishes priced between ¥750 and ¥850. Desserts and drinks are also available.

Port Discovery

This steampunk futuristic marina houses several unique attractions.

Nemo & Friends SeaRider

 Yes | 90cm | No | 5 minutes + pre-show | 30 to 45 minutes

This simulator-style attraction takes you on an undersea journey with Nemo and his friends. You will see characters from Finding Dory on your exciting adventure as you are shrunk down to the size of a fish.

This attraction does not warrant a wait of over 30 minutes in our opinion, so we recommend using Fastpass if possible, or waiting for the evening (5:30pm onwards) when waits are typically shorter.

Aquatopia

Take a seat on this wild, unpredictable adventure. Your watercraft will travel forwards, backward and spin in all directions – there is no set route, and the ride uses a trackless technology, so you never know where you are going next. You may even get a different route on different visits. Watch out for the waterfall!

Waits are shortest from 5:00 pm onwards, and we think this ride is best in the dark anyway.

 No | None | 2 minutes 30 seconds | 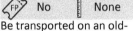 20 to 30 minutes

DisneySea Electric Railway

 No | None | No | 3 minutes 30 seconds | 5 to 15 minutes

Be transported on an old-timey overhead railway between the American Waterfront and Port Discovery. Get a unique perspective on these two fascinating lands of the Tokyo Disney Sea and save your feet.

The wait at Port Discovery is typically shorter than at the American Waterfront. If you choose to walk instead, this can be done in under 10 minutes.

Dining

Bayside Takeout – Snack location. Serves sushi rolls for ¥500, churros for ¥400, and drinks.
Breezeway Bites – Snack location. Serves fried pizza for ¥500, and drinks.
Horizon Bay Restaurant – Buffeteria location. Western cuisine. Entrees are ¥1150 to ¥1850 and include salmon, beef, hamburgers and chicken. Seasonal set menus may also be available.
Seaside Snacks – Snack location. Serves shrimp snacks for ¥500, and soft drinks.

American Waterfront

Be transported to the USA with touches both of New England and the big cities.

In addition to the attractions listed below, you can also find character meets at the **Village Greeting Place** in this area. Also, although not listed by the park as an attraction, you can explore the various decks of the **S.S. Columbia** ship on foot.

Big City Vehicles

Ride aboard a classic car from the early 20th century.

Let your vehicle take you down the street past the many shops, restaurants, and the giant S.S. Columbia.

There are several different vehicles for you to ride, including a police car and a delivery truck.

 No | None | ⓥ 5 to 10 minutes | ⌛ Less than 5 minutes

DisneySea Transit Steamer Line

 No | None | 📷 No | ⓥ 5 to 10 minutes | ⌛ 10 to 20 minutes

Get around Tokyo Disney Sea in style aboard a steamer. There are stops at Mediterranean Harbor, American Waterfront, and Lost River Delta.

Get a unique perspective on this beautiful park as you sail around and see corners of the park only visible from the steamers.

Operation stops during preparations for shows on the harbor and resumes after the performance.

Turtle Talk

This interactive show lets adults and kids speak to Crush and ask him questions about the turtle world; meanwhile, Crush has some questions for you about the human world. It's fun, and you might even learn to speak whale!

This attraction is presented entirely in Japanese, so you will likely want to skip it unless you can speak the language.

 No | None | ⓥ 15 minutes | ⌛ Until next show

Tower of Terror

FP Yes	102cm	📷 Yes	⌄ 6 minutes (incl. pre-show)	⧖ 100 to 150 minutes

The Tower of Terror starts as a walkthrough tour through the Hightower Hotel owned by Harrison Hightower III. When your tour guide takes you into Hightower's study, you see 'Shiriki Utundu,' a cursed wooden idol who you will encounter again when you board an elevator.

Expect to drop over 100ft again and again in this hair-raising ride. You can really feel the force of the elevator being pulled down faster than gravity, meaning you get lifted out of your seat. It is a slightly nicer feeling than free-fall drops, in our opinion. The motors on this ride are very powerful, and within a split-second, the elevator changes from going up to down. It really is a thrill.

Unlike the other versions of the Tower of Terror around the world, which are themed to The Twilight Zone or Guardians of the Galaxy, Tokyo DisneySea's Tower of Terror features this original story with all new interiors, theming and effects. The pre-show, in particular, is excellent.

We recommend a Fastpass to skip the lengthy waits, or riding in the last 30 minutes of the park's operating hours. Even with a Fastpass, you will likely wait 20 minutes or so to board the elevator, as there is no way to skip the queue between the pre-show and the actual ride.

Toy Story Mania

This is an interactive shooter attraction where each passenger in the car (in pairs, sat back-to-back) has a gun to shoot at interactive screens. It is great family fun, and each scene is different along the way.

Work hard to beat everyone else, but with a frantic urge to win, you may find that your arm aches after riding.

One of the resort's most popular attractions, Toy Story Mania, draws huge crowds while suffering from

FP Yes	None	⌄ 5 minutes 30 seconds	⧖ 120 to 180 minutes

a low hourly capacity. Your best bet is a Fastpass for this, riding it first thing at park opening, or within the last 30 minutes of park operation.

DisneySea Electric Railway

FP No	None	📷 No	⌄ 3 minutes 30 seconds	⏳ 10 to 20 minutes

Be transported on an old-timey overhead railway between the American Waterfront and Port Discovery. Get a unique perspective on these two fascinating lands of Tokyo DisneySea and save your feet.

The wait here is usually longer than at the station at Port Discovery. You can walk to Port Discovery in under 10 minutes if the wait here is too long.

Show: Big Band Beat at Broadway Music Theatre

This is the most popular daytime show at Tokyo DisneySea and is very different from the other shows. This Broadway-style spectacle includes musicians and dancers, as well as classic Disney characters. You will be surprised at Mickey's many talents, including drum playing and tap dancing!

On most days, the ticket lottery system is used for this show. The first show of the day is first-come-first-seated. Subsequent shows have unreserved seats at the balcony level and reserved seats at the orchestra level.

You will need to visit Biglietteria to attempt the ticket lottery – once inside, go to the touchscreen machine, follow the on-screen instructions (an English option is available): choose a show time, scan all your party's tickets, and then press the next button. If you win, a ticket will be printed out with your reserved seat number and performance time. You may only attempt the lottery once per day and must have all tickets present for each member of your party who wishes to view the show.

Show: Hello, New York!

This show, presented in the New York area of American Waterfront, features Mickey Mouse and friends enjoying the Big Apple. It is great fun with catchy music.

Dining

Barnacle Bill's – Snack location. Sells sausages with bones (¥380), alcohol (beer – ¥630), and non-alcoholic drinks.

Cape Cod Confections – Snack location. Sells sweets and souvenirs priced ¥470 to ¥1,000.

Cape Cop Cook-Off – Counter Service. Burgers are ¥600, or ¥990 as a meal. A low allergen menu is ¥770. Also serves nuggets and seafood chowder. Two 10-minute shows starring Duffy and friends (called 'My Friend Duffy') are performed here every 15 mins.

Delancey Catering – Snack location. Sells hot dogs for ¥450; also sells drinks.

Dockside Diner – Counter Service. Western cuisine. Sells fried chicken, roast beef sandwiches, and other individual items (¥750 to ¥800). A set meal is an extra ¥200-¥300.

High Tide Treats – Snack location. Sells churros for ¥350, also sells drinks.

Hudson River Harvest – Counter Service/Snack location. Sells seasonal snacks, and Mickey-shaped chocolate cream biscuits for ¥350, as well as drinks and desserts.

Liberty Landing Diner – Counter Service/Snack location. Sells pork rice rolls (¥500) and miso cream soup (¥320).

New York Deli – Counter Service. Bagels, sandwiches and paninis priced at ¥760 to ¥940 a la carte or ¥1150 to ¥1350 as a meal. Desserts, drinks and side items are also available.

Papadakis Fresh Fruit – Snack location. Sells drinks, snacks and fresh fruit cups (¥450).

Restaurant Sakura – Table Service. Seafood main courses are priced between ¥2080 to ¥2280. Side portions (¥500 to ¥620), drinks and desserts are also available.

S.S. Columbia Dining Room – Table Service. Western cuisine. Set menus are ¥3,700 to ¥7,600 including roast beef, sirloin steak, and fish dishes. A kids' set menu is ¥1,800.

The Teddy Roosevelt Lounge – Drinks lounge with snacks. Western cuisine. Serves alcoholic and non-alcoholic drinks. Appetizers are ¥410 to ¥1,000, sandwiches are about ¥1,320. Desserts are also available.

Lost River Delta

Explore this ancient civilization nestled within the remote Central American jungle.

DisneySea Transit Steamer Line

 No   None   No   5 to 10 minutes   15 to 20 minutes

Get around Tokyo Disney Sea in style aboard a steamer. There are stops at Mediterranean Harbor, American Waterfront, and Lost River Delta.

Get a unique perspective on this beautiful park as you sail around and see corners of the park only visible from the steamers.

Operation stops during preparations for shows on the harbor and resumes after the performance.

Indiana Jones Adventure: Temple of the Crystal Skull

Yes   117cm   Yes   3 minutes 30 seconds   60 to 90 minutes

Step into an adventure with Indiana Jones as you journey into the forbidden temple. Board your enhanced motion vehicle and become part of the action – be ready for evil curses, rolling boulders, snakes, bugs, spears, and much more on your treacherous journey.

A Single Rider line is available for this attraction, which will typically save you about 75% of the posted standby wait time. This is a near clone of the Indiana Jones attraction at Disneyland Resort in California, and it is one of the best attractions at the whole resort, in our opinion.

Note: The queue for this ride is relatively fast-moving, but it covers a lot of distance, so be prepared for a bit of a walk. Even in the Fastpass line, from handing in your Fastpass to loading could take 15 to 20 minutes.

Mickey and Friends Greeting Trails

There are three different trails in this area. At the end of the queue, you will have the chance to meet either Mickey, Minnie or Goofy in their explorer gear. A Disney photographer is available to take photos – you may also take your own photos.

Raging Spirits

FP Yes	117cm	📷 No	⌄ 2 minutes	⧖ 60 to 90 minutes

This rollercoaster ride will take you on an adventure through an ancient ceremonial site.

Your adventure will have you climbing, dropping, going around tight corners, and meandering in and around the ruins, even descending rapidly into a 360-degree loop as your mine cart goes out of control. The ride is a near-clone of a similar ride at Disneyland Paris, themed to Indiana Jones.

This is the most intense coaster at the resort, with the loop being particularly tight. It is a relatively short but fun experience. It is the only ride at the resort to go upside down.

As the ride has a loop, there are free 3-hour storage lockers available for use while on this attraction.

Saludos Amigos! Greeting Dock

You can meet Donald Duck in this Latin-themed corner of the park. A Disney photographer is available to take photos – you may also take your own photos.

"Song of Mirage" at Hangar Stage

This unique 30-minute Broadway-style show stars Mickey Mouse and his Disney Friends as they go on an adventure to seek out the Rio Dorado (Spanish for "golden river") and its legendary city of gold.

This show is performed in Japanese only, but it is still worth watching even if you do not speak the language as this is a fun show – some of the songs are in English, and the live singing is in English too.

Seating is available using the ticket lottery system. Visit Biglietteria to try your luck for a ticket. Non-reserved seating and standing areas are also available.

Dining

Expedition Eats – Snack location. Sells sausage dogs for ¥500.
Lost River Cookhouse – Snack location. Sells chicken legs for ¥500 each, as well as drinks.
Miguel's El Dorado Cantina – Counter Service. Mexican cuisine. Sells tacos, meat plates, seafood plates, quesadillas and more priced between ¥890 and ¥1,100 each. Also sells drinks and desserts.
Tropic Al's – Snack location. Sells tipo tortas (sweet-potato-style churros) for ¥350 each, also sells drinks.
Yucatan Base Camp Grill – Counter Service. Main courses are ¥1,050 to ¥1,260 including chicken, salmon or pork. A set menu is also available for ¥1,270 to 1,480 including a drink. The children's set menu is ¥940.

Arabian Coast

Experience the world of The Arabian Nights – keep an eye out for Aladdin.

Jasmine's Flying Carpets

FP No	None	📷 No	⌄ 1 minute 30 seconds	⧖ 10 to 20 minutes

Hop aboard one of Jasmine's magic carpets and fly across the Arabian Coast and Jasmine's garden. This is very similar to the Dumbo ride in its style but is typically less popular.

The way it differs from Dumbo is that as well as controlling how high you go on the carpets, you can also control the direction in which they tilt.

Sindbad's Storybook Voyage

FP No	None	📷 No	⌄ 10 minutes	⧖ 5 to 10 minutes

Board a boat and sail past scenes of Sindbad on one of his many exciting adventures on a relaxing boat cruise.

The concept of this ride is very similar to *"it's a small world"* at Tokyo Disneyland. It is family-friendly fun, and the animatronics' motions are incredibly lifelike!

This is one of the park's highlights for us – it has a great soundtrack, short waits, and is a cute experience overall.

Abu's Bazaar

This is listed as a shop on the DisneySea map, but we think it is an attraction.

Here you play one of two carnival-style games – if you win, you get to choose a Disney plush to take home; if you lose, you can choose a pin as a consolation prize. Either way, you do get something!

This activity is not free, and there is an extra charge (¥500).

It is popular with guests as the exclusive prizes change seasonally.

Look for the queue line in the area to join – expect to wait at least 30 minutes.

The Magic Lamp Theater

This popular attraction stars Genie from Disney's film Aladdin on an exciting 3D theater show adventure. The entire experience lasts about 20 minutes, including 11 minutes inside the main theater for the show. The main show is part live-show, part on-screen in Japanese, but you can ask for a translation device.

Be ready for a few surprises along the way as Shaban the Magician seeks to become the "world's greatest magician."

FP Yes | None | 11 minutes + pre-show | 30 to 45 minutes

Top Tip: Waits are long for this attraction during the day, but, in the evening, you can often walk straight into the next show.

Caravan Carousel

This is your standard fairground-style carousel, here themed to Aladdin's world.

The carousel is on two levels, which is rather unique – as you go around, you can enjoy the beautiful surroundings of this Port of Call.

FP No | None | 2 minutes | Less than 10 minutes

Dining

Casbah Food Court – Counter Service. Indian cuisine. Sells curry dishes with meat or fish, naan and rice. Dishes are ¥840 to ¥1,300. Side salads, desserts and drinks are also available.
Open Sesame – Snack location. Sells mickey churros and drinks priced between ¥200 and ¥400.
Sultan's Oasis – Snack location. Sells desserts, snacks (curry buns), drinks, soup and ice creams priced between ¥300 to ¥500.

Mermaid Lagoon

Explore the world of Ariel, the Little Mermaid. This area of the park is almost entirely indoors and perfect for cold and rainy days. Most of the rides here are targeted towards younger children – this is the equivalent of Fantasyland in Tokyo Disneyland.

Flounder's Flying Fish Coaster

This is a great starter rollercoaster for kids as it is relatively tame and doesn't get up to too much speed.

Here you can see Flounder (from The Little Mermaid) and his friends who will welcome you aboard to whizz around and over the lagoon.

| FP | No | 90cm | 1 minute | 15 to 30 minutes |

Scuttle's Scooters

| FP | No | None | 📷 No | ✓ 1 minute | Less than 20 minutes |

Sit inside a hermit crab and get ready to go for a wild spin. This is a standard fairground-style ride where the cars spin around a central object and go up and down as they go around.

Jumpin' Jellyfish

| FP | No | None | 📷 No | ✓ 1 minute | Less than 15 minutes |

Glide gently up and down on a jellyfish in this indoor attraction.

Blowfish Balloon Race

Board your seashell gondola (carried by a blowfish) and go for an underwater spin.

This is a fairly standard slow-spinning attraction.

| FP | No | 90cm | 1 minute | 15 to 30 minutes |

Ariel's Playground

This indoor playground features a variety of different areas from turtles who "spit" water to a spinning ship's wheel, and even an indoor ropes course. Cast Members hand out exploration maps so you can enjoy Ariel's Playground to the fullest.

The Whirlpool

This is a standard fairground-style teacup ride, but here you sit in cups made out of "kelp" (algae) instead.

Watch out for the other guests as you are spun around by a whirlpool.

Use the wheel in the center to spin faster.

| FP No | None | 1 minute 30 seconds | Less than 20 minutes |

Ariel's Greeting Grotto

Meet Ariel in her underwater world for a chat, autograph, and even a photo. You may take your own photos. A professional Disney photographer is also present too during your meet-and-greet with the Little Mermaid herself.

This meet and greet is scheduled to close on 31st March 2020 permanently – no replacement has been announced at the time of writing.

Show: "King Triton's Concert" at Mermaid Lagoon Theater

This 14-minute circus-style show stars Ariel and her friends with incredible singing, acrobats and puppetry, above and around you. With moments including songs such as "Under the Sea" and "Part of Your World" you are sure to be singing along.

Please note the show is entirely in Japanese, but you can ask a Cast Member for a translation device in English. The show uses a Fastpass ticketing system for reserved seats, or you can simply walk in – honestly, you shouldn't need the Fastpass the vast majority of the time and can simply join the next show.

Dining

Sebastian's Calypso Kitchen – Counter Service. Sells pizzas and calzones for ¥670 to ¥720, and set menus for ¥1,060 to ¥1,100. Desserts and drinks are also available.

Mysterious Island

Mysterious Island contains the park's iconic volcano and is the centerpiece of Tokyo DisneySea. In this steampunk-style land you can discover the secrets deep within the Earth and under the sea at Captain Nemo's hidden base.

Journey to the Center of the Earth

Travel to the Center of the Earth with Captain Nemo on board one of his unique vehicles. Your adventure will be filled with surprises around every corner, including lightning and fire.

The story is relatively bewildering, and there is not a huge amount of action for most of the ride, but the theming is to be admired.

However, be careful, because if the volcano erupts during your visit, you will need to get out quickly. This roller coaster-like escape has you hitting

| FP | Yes | 117cm | 3 minutes | 90 to 150 minutes |

speeds of 75km/h.

This is by far one of the resort's most popular attractions, and Fastpasses run out very quickly. You should make this a priority during your visit.

20,000 Leagues Under the Sea

Captain Nemo wants to take you on yet another adventure – this time, you will board a submarine and venture under the sea in search of the lost city of Atlantis. This is a unique and fun ride that is sure to awaken the explorer in you.

Despite being original, we don't think this attraction warrants a long wait – ride this at the start of the day, or after 6:00 pm for waits of 15 minutes or less.

| FP | Yes | None | 5 minutes | 30 to 45 minutes |

Dining

Refreshment Station – Snack location. Sells potato churros for ¥450.
Nautilus Galley – Snack location. Sells gyoza dogs (¥500), and assorted snacks priced between ¥380 and ¥500 each. This location also offers seasonal items.
Vulcania Restaurant – Counter Service. Chinese cuisine. Main dishes such as shrimp, tofu, deep fried chicken and sour pork are ¥980. Sides such as dim sum (¥420), spring rolls (¥320) and salads (¥420) are also available. A 2-course set menu is ¥1,880. The kid's menu is ¥940, and there are also two low allergen menus at ¥820 and ¥1040.

Tokyo DisneySea Park Entertainment

Fantasmic! (Closes 25th March, 2020)

The highlight of any night at Tokyo DisneySea is likely to be *Fantasmic!*, a stunning nighttime spectacular taking place on the lagoon of the Mediterranean Harbor. Who could be a more magical star of the show than Sorcerer Mickey, of course? Various parade-like floats sail across the waters, and giant set pieces make this a visually stunning show to watch. You can expect to see favorite Disney characters, giant screens, fire, lasers, and pyrotechnics.

In our opinion, this is, by far, the best nighttime show at the resort and a truly magical end to the night.

Guests will often bring blankets with them to mark out their personal space and sit on these 2 hours or longer before the performance begins for the best spots. However, good views of the show are available from all around the Mediterranean Harbor area of the park, so you do not need to arrive too far in advance if you do not mind being a row or two from the front and seeing the show from angle - the ideal viewing location is from near the Hotel MiraCosta. The show's duration is approximately 20 minutes.

Important Note: This show will close on 25th March 2020. At the time of writing, a replacement show has not been announced.

Touring Plans

Touring plans are easy-to-follow guides that minimize your waiting time in queue lines throughout the day. By following them, you can maximize your time in the parks and experience more attractions. There are several different touring plans available to suit your needs.

To see all of Tokyo Disneyland, you will need to allocate at least two days. However, you can hit the headline attractions at the park in just one day if you are pressed for time. The same applies to Tokyo DisneySea, where two days are preferable, but the highlights can be experienced in one day. An ideal length of a trip to take everything in at a more leisurely pace would be 5 or 6 days.

These touring plans are not set in stone, so feel free to adapt them to the needs of your party. It is important to note that these plans focus on experiencing the rides; if your focus is on meeting all the characters or seeing all the shows, then a touring plan is unlikely to be suitable for you. The only way to minimize waits for characters is to get to the parks and meet-and-greets early. The two-day touring plans in this section do include some shows, however, and allow more time for flexibility.

These touring plans are intense, BUT you will get to cram in as much as possible during your visit. Getting up early and being at the park before opening is a must – your first 30 minutes will set you up for the rest of the day.

If you do not want to experience a particular ride, skip that step but do not change the order of the steps. If an attraction is closed for refurbishment during your trip, skip that step.

You must purchase your tickets in advance to make the most of your time and these touring plans. If you need to buy a ticket on the day, turn up at least 45 minutes earlier than the recommended start times on these plans - and even earlier during peak season.

Insider Tip: To minimize the time you spend waiting in queue lines, you will often need to cross the park from one side to the other – this is purposely done by theme parks to disperse crowds more evenly.

Important Note on Tickets: Unlike other Disney resorts, if you buy a one-day ticket, there is no option to visit both theme parks on the same day. If you buy a 2-Day ticket, then you will need to choose one park per day; on a 3-Day ticket, you are limited to one park for each of the first two days, and then can park-hop on the third day. If you wish to go between the two parks from day one, then you will need to stay at a Disney hotel and buy the special multi-day ticket from the hotel itself. There is no way to use a one-day ticket to visit both parks on the same day. For this guide and making the most of your time, you should stick to one park each day.

1-Day Plan at Tokyo Disneyland – Until 14th April 2020

1: Arrive at the park gates at least 30 minutes before the start of Happy15. Pick up a Park Map and a Today Times Guide in World Bazaar. The Today Times Guide lists parade, show, character, and firework times, as well as attraction closures.

2: One ride will be open during this Happy15. Until Spring 2020, this will be *Buzz Lightyear's Astro Blasters*. Ride this first.

3: Backtrack slightly and get a Fastpass for *Monsters, Inc. Ride & Go Seek*.

4: Head to *Pooh's Hunny Hunt* and ride this now. You should be on the ride within 30 minutes, which will likely be the shortest wait this ride will have all day.

5: Ride *Haunted Mansion* in Fantasyland.

6: Ride *Splash Mountain*. Use Single Rider to save yourself a lot of time.

7: Assuming both Fastpasses are still available, you will need to decide whether you wish to grab a Fastpass for *Big Thunder Mountain* or *Space Mountain*.

8: Is it time to use your *Monsters Inc.* Fastpass yet? Work this around your lunch plans.

9: It's likely time for lunch now. Have a Counter Service meal to save you time. Fastpass will have run out for most rides by now, except maybe *Star Tours*.

10: Ride *Star Tours* if the wait is under 30 minutes. If not, you can do this later. You have now done most of the major attractions that offer Fastpass.

11: Go to *Tomorrowland Hall* and try the lottery for one of the park's shows. Good luck.

12: Ride *Pirates of the Caribbean*.

13: Note the time of the park's daily parade and make time for this. We recommend experiencing the parade in the hub area in front of Cinderella Castle. Get there at least 30 minutes before the start time.

14: You now have the afternoon free to take in the rides and shows that are of most interest to you. We recommend the following Disney classics: *Peter Pan's Flight*, *"it's a small world"* and *Jungle Cruise*.

15: Don't forget to use your *Big Thunder Mountain* or *Space Mountain* Fastpass.

16: Enjoy the evening entertainment – this varies but may include the *Dreamlights* nighttime parade, fireworks, or even a projection show on Cinderella Castle.

17: If you are staying right until the end of the day, the park usually empties significantly in the last 30 minutes before closing – this can be your chance to ride one of the park's big rides that you missed but without the wait – or re-ride a favorite of yours. If a ride has a very long wait at the end of the day (over 1 hour), the standby queue line may close before the park closing time.

Note: Guests who do not have Happy15 entry should skip step 2 – everything else remains the same. Guests without Happy15 entry should be at the park at least 45 minutes before regular park opening on weekends.

1-Day Plan at Tokyo Disneyland – From 15th April 2020

1: Arrive at the park gates at least 30 minutes before the start of Happy15. Pick up a Park Map and a Today Times Guide in World Bazaar. The Today Times Guide lists parade, show, character, and firework times, as well as attraction closures.

2: One ride will be open during this Happy15. From 15th April 2020, this will be *Enchanted Tale of Beauty and the Beast*. Do not ride this now, but instead get a Fastpass to ride this later.

3: Head to *Pooh's Hunny Hunt*. Ride this straight away. You should be here before the park officially opens to other guests.

4: Ride *Space Mountain* – this involves some backtracking, but by riding this early in the day, you can avoid long waits later.

5: Ride *Haunted Mansion* in Fantasyland.

6: Ride *Splash Mountain*. Use Single Rider to save yourself a lot of time.

7: If you can reserve another Fastpass, then now is the perfect time to grab a Fastpass for *Monsters, Inc. Ride & Go Seek*. If that is not available, then grab a Fastpass for *Big Thunder Mountain*.

8: Is it time to use your *Enchanted Tale of Beauty and the Beast* Fastpass yet? Work this around lunch.

9: It's likely time for lunch now. Have a Counter Service meal to save you time. Fastpass will have run out for most rides by now, except maybe *Star Tours*.

10: Ride *Star Tours* if the wait is under 30 minutes. If not, you can do this later. You have now done most of the major attractions that offer Fastpass.

11: Go to T*omorrowland Hall* and try the lottery for one of the park's shows.

12: Ride *Pirates of the Caribbean*.

13: Note the time of the park's daily parade and make time for this. We recommend experiencing the parade in the hub area in front of Cinderella Castle. Get there at least 30 minutes before the start time.

14: You now have the afternoon free to take in the rides and shows that are of most interest to you. We recommend the following Disney classics: *Peter Pan's Flight*, *"it's a small world"* and *Jungle Cruise*.

15: Don't forget to use your *Monsters, Inc. Ride & Go Seek* or *Big Thunder Mountain* Fastpass.

16: Enjoy the evening entertainment – this varies but may include the Dreamlights nighttime parade, fireworks, or even a projection show on Cinderella Castle.

17: If you are staying until the end of the day, the park usually empties significantly in the last 30 minutes before closing – this can be your chance to ride one of

the park's big rides that you may have missed but without the wait – or re-ride a favorite of yours. If a ride has a very long wait at the end of the day (over 1 hour), the standby queue line may close before the park closing time.

Note: Guests without Happy15 entry should follow the same strategy. If Fastpass has already run out by the time you reach *Enchanted Tale of Beauty and the Beast* (this could happen if many guests are ahead of you early in the morning), then go to *Pooh's Hunny Hunt* first to get a Fastpass. After that, ride *Enchanted Tale of Beauty and the Beast* using the Single Rider queue line, then continue from Step 5 (skip *Space Mountain* unless the wait is under 30 minutes). Guests without Happy15 entry should be at the park at least 45 minutes before regular park opening on weekends.

2-Day Plan at Tokyo Disneyland – Day One

1: Arrive at the park gates at least 15 minutes before the start of Happy15 if you have access to this. If not, be at the park gates at least 30 minutes before the park opens. Pick up a Park Map and a Today Times Guide in World Bazaar. The Today Times Guide lists parade, show, character, and firework times, as well as attraction closures.

2: Go to *Monsters, Inc. Ride & Go Seek* and get a Fastpass.

3: Head to *Pooh's Hunny Hunt*. Ride this now.

4: Ride *Space Mountain* – this involves some backtracking, but by riding this early in the day, you can avoid long waits later on.

5: Go to *Tomorrowland Hall* and try the lottery for tickets to a show. If it is time for your *Monsters, Inc. Ride & Go Seek* Fastpass to be used, do so now.

6: Ride *Haunted Mansion* in Fantasyland. Grab a Fastpass for *Big Thunder Mountain*.

7: Most seasons have a morning mini-parade, go and watch this.

8: Use your *Monsters, Inc. Ride & Go Seek* Fastpass if you have not yet done so.

9: Ride *Pirates of the Caribbean*.

10: Fit lunch around your

Fastpass plans.

11: Experience the attractions in Adventureland, including *Jungle Cruise, Swiss Family Treehouse, The Enchanted Tiki Room,* and *Western River Railroad*.

12: Note the time of the park's daily afternoon parade and make time for this. We recommend experiencing the parade in the hub area in front of Cinderella Castle. Get there at least 30 minutes before the start time.

13: If it is time, use your *Big Thunder Mountain* Fastpass.

14: Explore the rest of Westernland, including *Country Bear Theater, Mark Twain Riverboat,* and *Tom Sawyer Island Rafts*.

15: Enjoy the evening entertainment – this varies but may include the Dreamlights nighttime parade, fireworks, or even a projection show on Cinderella Castle. Fit dinner around this.

16: If you are staying right until the end of the day, the park usually empties significantly in the last 30 minutes before closing – this can be your chance to ride one of the park's big rides that you may have missed but without the wait – or re-ride a favorite of yours. If a ride has a very long wait at the end of the day (over 1 hour), the standby queue line may close before the park closing time.

This plan covers around half the park's major attractions and many of the smaller ones. Follow Day 2 to see the rest.

Note: Guests without Happy15 entry should be at the park at least 45 minutes before regular park opening on weekends.

2-Day Plan at Tokyo Disneyland – Day Two

1: Arrive at the park gates at least 15 minutes before the start of Happy15 if you have access to this. If not, be at the park gates 30 minutes before the park opens. Pick up a Park Map and a Today Times Guide in World Bazaar. The Today Times Guide lists parade, show, character, and firework times, as well as attraction closures.

2: Go to *Enchanted Tale of Beauty and the Beast* and get a Fastpass to ride later in the day.

3: Go to *Pooh's Hunny Hunt* and ride this now. Even though you did this yesterday, we feel this attraction is worth experiencing twice. Alternatively, you can swap this for *Monsters Inc. Ride & Go Seek*.

4: Ride *Buzz Lightyear's Astro Blasters*. Go via *Tomorrowland Hall* if you want to try for a show lottery ticket.

5: Ride *Splash Mountain* - if the queue is long (it shouldn't be this early in the day), consider using the Single Rider queue line to reduce your wait time significantly.

6: Experience *Beaver Brothers Explorer Canoes*.

7: Tackle Fantasyland's many attractions. Start with *Peter Pan's Flight,* then *Dumbo the Flying Elephant*. If you enjoyed *Haunted Mansion* yesterday, feel free to re-ride.

8: Have lunch at *Queen of*

Hearts Banquet Hall; work this around your *Enchanted Tale of Beauty and the Beast* Fastpass.

9: Explore the rest of Fantasyland, including *Cinderella's Fairy Tale Hall, Pinocchio's Daring Journey,* and *Mickey's Philharmagic*.

10: If you want to watch the main afternoon parade, make time for this around now. We recommend experiencing the parade in the hub area in front of Cinderella Castle. Get there at least 30 minutes before the start time.

11: Explore *Toontown* and all its attractions – the character meets here can get huge waits, so do be aware of this.

12: Continue round to Tomorrowland and ride *Star Tours* and watch *Stitch Encounter*.

13: Enjoy the evening entertainment – this varies but may include the *Dreamlights* nighttime parade, fireworks, or even a projection show on

Cinderella Castle. Fit dinner around this.

14: If you are staying right until the end of the day, the park usually empties significantly in the last 30 minutes before closing – this can be your chance to ride one of the park's big rides that you may have missed but without the wait – or re-ride a favorite of yours.

With this plan, you should comfortably cover the rest of the park on your second day.

Note: The above plan works for both guests who do and do not have Happy15. Guests with Happy15 entry should ride whichever ride is available to them during this period (e.g., *Buzz Lightyear's Astro Blasters* or *Enchanted Tale of Beauty and the Beast* – this changes periodically) on both days.

Note: Guests without Happy15 entry should be at the park at least 45 minutes before regular park opening on weekends and public holidays.

1-Day Plan at Tokyo DisneySea

1: Arrive at the park gates at least 30 minutes before the start of Happy15 if you have access to this. If not, be at the park gates 30 minutes before the park opens. Pick up a Park Map and a Today Times Guide. The Today Times Guide lists parade, show, character, and firework times, as well as attraction closures.

2: Head straight to *Soaring: Fantastic Flight*. Grab a Fastpass.

3: Go to *Journey to the Center of the Earth*. Ride this iconic attraction.

4: Next door is *20,000 Leagues Under the Sea*. Ride this now.

5: Ride *Sindbad's Storybook Voyage* in the Arabian Coast.

6: Make your way to Lost River Delta. Ride *Raging Spirits* using Single Rider.

7: Ride *Indiana Jones Adventure*. If the wait is longer than 30 minutes, use Single Rider.

8: Keep an eye on your *Soaring* Fastpass — if it is time to use it, head back now.

9: Cross the park using the *DisneySea Transit Steamer Line* to the American Waterfront.

Before doing this, consult the TDR app or website to check Fastpasses are still available for Tower of Terror.

10: Get a *Tower of Terror* Fastpass.

11: Time for lunch.

12: Visit *Biglietteria* and try the lottery to see if you win a spot to watch *Big Band Beat*.

13: Ride the *Venetian Gondolas*. If you haven't yet used your *Soaring* Fastpass, is it now time?

14: Ride *DisneySea Electric Railway* to Port Discovery.

15: Ride *Aquatopia* and *Nemo and Friends SeaRider*.

16: Keep an eye on both your *Tower of Terror* Fastpass and (if you have it) your *Big Band Beat* show time. In the meantime, feel free to explore *Fortress Explorations* and do the *Leonardo Challenge*.

17: Enjoy the evening entertainment – this varies but may include the *Fantasmic* nighttime show, fireworks, or other entertainment — fit dinner around this.

18 If you are staying until the end of the day, the park usually empties significantly in the last 30 minutes before closing – this can be your chance to ride one of the park's big rides that you may have missed but without the wait – or re-ride a favorite of yours. This could be the way to do *Toy Story Mania!* without waiting for two hours.

2-Day Plan at Tokyo DisneySea

With a two-day plan, follow Day 1 as above.

For Day 2, get to the park 30 minutes before opening and grab a Fastpass for either *Toy Story Mania* or *Tower of Terror,* and ride the other immediately after. For the rest of the day, re-ride your favorites from Day 1, and explore Arabian Coast in more detail, and Mermaid's Lagoon, which was not visited on Day 1.

You can use Day 2 to go for a fantastic meal at Magellan's too either at lunch or dinner and take in the daytime shows.

Note: Guests without Happy15 entry should be at the park at least 45 minutes before regular park opening on weekends.

Ikspiari

When arriving at Tokyo Disney Resort by train at JR Maihama station, if you turn left, you will be at Ikspiari, a shopping center with a large variety of places to eat and shop. There are also activities here. You can also access Ikspiari by taking the Disney Resort Line monorail to Resort Gateway Station.

Generally speaking, Ikspiari is open from 10:00 am to 10:00 pm daily, although individual store hours may differ. *Ikspiari* is split across multiple levels.

There is an ATM run by 7Bank located on the first floor, which will accept foreign credit and debit cards. There is also an ATM run by Japan Post Bank on the second floor. There are a further two ATMs, but these generally do not accept foreign cards.

Deals for international guests:
International guests should be sure to stop by the *Ikspiari* Information Counter and show their passport for a free Welcome Card, which offers a variety of discounts in selected stores and restaurants –usually, these are 5% or 10%.

Over 40 shops also offer tax-free shopping for foreigners (the tax is usually 10% on goods) – the minimum purchase is ¥5,000 per store (excluding tax) – the tax will be deducted immediately.

Dining - Japanese

- **Ichizenya Ikspiari Kitchen** – Counter Service. Broiled charcoal-fired pork served in a 'Donburi' style.
- **Ippudo** – Table Service. Ramen restaurant.
- **Komeraku** – Table Service. Rice soup, fried chicken, rice bowls and much more.
- **Kyo No Uta** – An all-you-can-eat buffet serving dishes made from seasonal vegetables and carefully selected ingredients.
- **Mai Chibo** – Table Service. Teppanyaki restaurant.
- **Rin-ya** – Offers Japanese cuisine made with seasonal ingredients, such as the signature "Hegisoba," made with kneaded seaweed. You can also enjoy carefully selected locally brewed sake and snacks to complement them.
- **Shabu-Shabu Tajimaya Ikspiari Store** – Table Service. Shabu-shabu dishes.
- **Shinkenshoubu Ikspiari Kitchen** – Counter Service. Specializes in Miso ramen noodles.
- **Sukiyaki Ningyocho Imahan** – Table Service. The interior of our restaurant is inspired by the design of an Edo-period house. Enjoy world-famous Japanese food, such as sukiyaki and grilled steak from the best grade Japanese black beef.
- **Tonkatsu Wako** – Specializes in pork cutlets.
- **Tsukiji Ginndaco** – Snack location. Serves Edo-style octopus dumplings.
- **Tsukiji Tamasushi** – A long-established Edomae Sushi restaurant which opened its first store in Tsukiji in 1924. Offers authentic sushi at a reasonable price using fresh

ingredients shipped directly from the Tsukiji Market.
- **Uminchu Shubo** – Table Service. Feast on island cuisine, made with Okinawan ingredients, along with 40 different kinds of awamori (an alcoholic drink).
- **Yotsubanoka Iskpiari Kitche** – Counter Service. Sanuki-udon noodle with Soy sauce made in Kagawa, and the mild and tasty stock from dried small sardines in Setouchi.

Dining - Western

- **Bar Rica Cerveza** – Table Service. Spanish bar serving drinks and pinchos.
- **Buffet The Grace** – Buffet-style restaurant with Western dishes.
- **Café Kaila** - Taste the popular Hawaiian-inspired pancakes, waffles, and omelettes for breakfast. As well as this, you can enjoy pasta, sandwiches, and the special Ikspiari menu.
- **Guzman Y Gomez** – Counter Service. A premium Mexican fast-food restaurant born in Australia.
- **Kafe Trail & Track** – Café and restaurant specializing in Hamburg steaks.
- **Maihama Youshokuken Iskpiari Kitchen** – Counter Service. Cooked-to-order omelets.
- **Mare Cucina** – Table Service. Casual Italian fare.
- **Omusubi Gonbei** – Counter service. Freshly polished, freshly boiled and freshly prepared rice balls starting at ¥100 including tax. Also offers toasted rice balls.
- **Outback Steakhouse** – Table Service. American casual dining, specializing in steaks.
- **Pitta 00** – Genuine Neapolitan pizza officially

recognized by the AVPN (Associazione Verace Pizza Napoletana)!
- **Rainforest Café** – Table Service. The first of its kind in Japan. Thunder roars in the sky, birdsong rings out, and elephants, gorillas, and colorful fish move around as if they were the real things.
- **Red Lobster** – Table Service. American seafood restaurant. Also serves steak, pizza, pasta, paella, and even has a special menu for kids.
- **Rio Grande Grill** – Table Service. Specializes in Brazilian BBQ (churrasco), with a variety of cuts of meat including beef and seafood, skewered and grilled in a specialized oven.
- **Rocky's Ikspiari Kitchen** –

Counter Service. Generous helpings of beefsteak and Hamburg steak roasted on a hot iron plate. Choose your favorite sauce, and eat your fill!
- **Roti's House** – Enjoy a variety of craft beers made by sharp and skilled craftspeople, with food to accompany.
- **Susan's Meat Ball** – Counter Service. Choose your favorite meat and sauce to make your very own original meatballs! Enjoy American home cooking at this New York-style meatball restaurant.
- **TGI Fridays** – Table Service. Popular American comfort food.

Dining - Asian (Non-Japanese)

- **Haochaoz** – Snack location. Serves dim sum and Chinese dumplings.
- **Ishiyaki Bibimbap Babi** – Have a fresh hot Ishiyaki (stone-grilled) Bibimbap made just for you with your choice of toppings.
- **Monsoon Café** – Table Service. Taste the healthy ethnic dishes selected from the menus of various Asian countries with a "relaxed

Oriental" atmosphere.
- **Seiryumon** – Table Service. A restaurant based on the idea of creating the atmosphere of the night market and of Taiwan's most popular eating establishments. Offers jiaozi, dim sum, stewed pork, and minced pork rice, served on small dishes.
- **Shoufukuchubou** – Counter Service. In the

atmosphere of a busy Chinese food stall, you can taste Chinese dishes. Offers various Chinese menus including the Sichuan dish "Sichuan Mabo doufu."
- **Toraji** – Table Service. A modern take on a Korean traditional house "Hanok" - offers not only Korean-style grilled meat, but also Korean home-cooked dishes at reasonable prices.

Dining - Bars and Cafes

• **A Le Loic** – "Sophisticated and cute" gelato & crepe shop inspired by beautiful Paris streets.
• **Café Chez Madu** – A bakery café, home to delicious, fresh-baked bread and pastries.
• **Gong Cha** – Taiwan-style tea in a casual setting.
• **Honolulu Coffee** – Uses carefully selected Kona coffee beans that can be harvested only in the Kona district of Hawaii. Kona coffee has less of a bitter taste and more of a soft tartness. The coffee goes well with the popular traditional pancake.

• **Kua'aina** – Serves Hawaiian-style hamburgers and sandwiches.
• **Nana's Green Tea** – Sweets and drinks made with macha from Kyoto and high quality Hojicha.
• **Pie Face** – Traditional Australian meat pies filled with good ingredients. Also offers drinks, such as roast coffee imported directly from Australia.
• **Starbucks Coffee** – World-famous coffee chain.
• **Old Owl** – A British-style pub.
• **Torcedor** – A British-style cigar bar.
• **Tully's Coffee** – A specialty

coffee shop from Seattle which provides real coffee with an emphasis on quality. There is also a range of side dishes to go well with your coffee, including sandwiches and Danish pastries.

Dining - Sweets and Snacks

• **Bake Cheese Tart** – These lightly-salted tarts combine a special mousse (blended from three varieties of cheese) with a twice-baked cookie, to give a crispy-yet-soft texture. Also serves ice cream.
• **Godiva** – High quality and richly flavored products such as pralines and truffles, as well as seasonal collections, baked goods, ice

creams and their signature chocolate drink, "chocolixir."
• **Krispy Kreme Doughnuts** – Doughnuts made by a recipe which has been kept secret for over 70 years. Also serves coffee.
• **Lola's Cupcakes Tokyo** – Beautiful handcrafted cupcakes from this London-based brand.
• **Manneken** – The first Belgian waffle shop in

Japan. Freshly-made waffles over the counter.
• **Nihonnbashi Nishikihorin** – Serves karinto (fried dough cake) in 9 flavors.
• **Paradis/Arinco** – A combined shop consisting of "PARADIS," a popular pastry shop, and "ARINCO," a Swiss roll specialist whose main shop is in Kyoto.

Dining - Food Shops

• **Glocal Food Bazaar** – A specialist food shop with a line-up of goods, both homegrown and imported.
• **Lupicia** – Fresh tea (black, green, oolong, and others) imported from overseas, as well as sweets and utensils which go along with the tea.
• **Seijo Ishii** – A supermarket-style place

that offers a wide range of items, including fresh foods, imported wines and cheese, as well as various home-made deli products and desserts. A great place to get a cheap bento box-style meal – from one hour before closing, these are heavily discounted.

Shops - Clothing

• **B: Ming: Life Store By Beams** – Men's and women's clothing for casual and business occasions, as well as kids' clothing.
• **Breeze** – A kidswear shop.
• **Çayhane** – Clothing and fashion goods inspired by various ethnic cultures.
• **Ciaopanic** – Casual clothes for ladies and men.
• **Coco Deal** – A casual brand for active ladies with an eye for new fashions.
• **Collage Gallardagalante** – Ladies fashion.
• **Diesel** – Premium casual brand with a wide range of items including denims and fashion goods.
• **E Hyphen World Gallery** – Ladies fashion.
• **Earth Music & Ecology Head Store** – Stocks the "earth music & ecology" brand as well as other trendy, casual clothes for daily use, as well as kids' clothing and maternity wear.
• **F.i.n.t** – Combines both 60's vintage style and the latest trends.
• **Gap/Gap Kids** – Based on the concept of "simple and clean," Gap offers clothing in a wide range of sizes for men, women, kids and babies.
• **Go! Go! Laundry** – A unisex brand, focusing on T-shirts infused with a sense of playfulness.
• **Graniph** – A T-shirt shop that offers "T-shirt meets Art."
• **Guess** – The lifestyle brand from LA, which stands

for a sexy, young, adventurous attitude. It has developed its sophisticated collection over 30 years.
• **Lacoste** – A French brand established in 1933. Find sporty and the comfortable clothes with a modern design in this "lifestyle" brand.
• **Local Motion** – A brand from Hawaii with a wide range of casual clothing and lifestyle goods, including surfer-style and clothes for daily life.
• **Lowrys Farm** – Ladieswear with a range of basic, casual goods infused with a hint of current trends.
• **Natural Anthem** – Outdoor goods, travel items, west coast beach style and clothes for daily use.
• **Niko and...** – A general lifestyle store with men's and women's clothes, and interior items, all designed for your needs.
• **Pageboy** – Women's casual wear.
• **Rive Droite** – Women's casual wear.
• **Ropé Picnic/Vis** – ROPÉ

PICNIC is a casual French brand. ViS is the shop for "grown-up girls" who are aware of the latest trends.
• **Te Chichi** – Cute, sweet goods which combine a basic, classic design with modern trends.
• **Tommy Hilfiger** – A rich collection of American preppy products suitable for many situations.
• **United Arrows Green Label Relaxing** – Men's, women's, and kids' clothing & accessories.
• **Urban Research Doors** – Well-designed, long-life, environmentally-friendly goods. As well as comfortable clothes for ladies, men, and kids, there is a collection of general goods, like furniture and containers.
• **Wash Wash** – Women's wear.
• **Wego** – A "mix used style," blending together used items selected from all over the world, new and fashionable original items, and selected items.

Shops - Accessories

- **ABC Mart** – A specialty store for shoes, with many types of shoes to choose from: new and classically designed sneakers, for women, for business, for kids, and more.
- **Amo's Style by Triumph** – Intimate apparel for ladies.
- **Ane Mone** – An accessories and bag shop with a European city vibe.
- **Archimedes Spiral** – A watch shop from antiques to the latest models.
- **Claire's** – The world's largest accessory chain.
- **Doctor Belee** – A shop specializing in neckties and shirts.
- **Flag** – Women's shoes.
- **Haruta** – Traditional-style shoes.
- **Its' Demo** – A fashion convenience store selling clothes, accessories, cosmetics, fashion goods, snacks and drinks.
- **Jins** – Eyewear and sunglasses shop.
- **Kaneko Optical Kaneko Gankyo** – Eyewear and sunglasses shop.
- **Kinuya** – Socks, gloves, scarves and accessories.
- **Kura Chika by Porter** – Bags and fashion goods made in Japan.
- **Lazy Susan** – A wide range of items, including bags, fragrances, and lifestyle goods.
- **Maison de Fleur** – French-style high quality items for women.
- **Mother House** – Mother House produces bags, jewelry, shoes, and shirts in five countries for both men and women.
- **Mare Mare Daily Market** – This natural shop, which invokes the impression of a French house, offers casual shoes, mules, and sandals.
- **Override** – A hat shop based on the concept of "Japanese modern."
- **Randa Luculiana** – Ladies shoes.
- **Samantha Vega & chouette gallery** – A combined shop of Samantha Vega and Samantha & chouette. The former offers useful and fashionable bags in a "mature casual" style. The latter offers bags pursuing a simple, elegant luxury.
- **Une Nana Cool** – Ladies underwear.

Shops - Jewelry

- **4oC** – Sells jewelry and watches which prioritize comfort, and brightly colored bags.
- **Aqua Silver** – Silver accessories made by a craftsman at a studio in Shibuya.
- **Ete** – Simple jewelry, with a hint of playfulness hidden in the design.
- **Folli Follie** – With the philosophy "affordable, fashionable luxury," this shop's items are popular with women all over the world.
- **Star Jewelry** – Craftsmen with traditional skills work together with designers to create the beautiful jewelry sold here.
- **The Kiss & Pair Ring Café** – Specializes in matching accessories for couples.

Shops - Hobbies & Household Goods

- **Asoko+3Coins** – A collaboration between "3COINS", a variety store selling useful and trendy products, and "ASOKO", a variety shop selling pop-design goods based on the concept of "let's enjoy surprises!
- **Carta Scopio** – Sells highly collectible items, including trading cards, movie-related goods and smoking supplies.
- **Charis Seijo** – "Charis" means "blessing" or "gift" in Greek. Offers the gifts of nature such as high quality essential oils and aromatherapy items.
- **Cuccuma** – Makes flower arrangements one-by-one with care.
- **Disney Store** – The largest Disney Store in Japan. Sells several items that are only available here.
- **Maruzen** – Bookshop with a catalogue including titles in both Japanese and foreign languages.
- **Natural Kitchen &** – Offers useful daily goods, starting

at ¥100. The range goes from the kitchen, to the bathroom and other areas.
• **Plaza** – Imported products from across the world.
• **Quatre Saisons** – This shop offers furniture and interior goods made of natural materials.
• **Shinseido** – A CD and DVD shop.
• **Stone World Premium Store** – A shop featuring natural rocks, jewelry, and accessories.
• **Timeless Comfort** – Interior and home goods.
• **Yorozuya Jyugoya** – Gifts ranging from desserts to stationery and knick-knacks made from Echizen paper.

Shops - Health & Beauty

• **Atelier Haruka** – Beauty salon with hair and makeup.
• **Bird in Nail by Atelier Haruka** – Nail salon.
• **Eyelash Salon Blanc** – A beauty shop, specializing in eyelashes and eyebrows.
• **L'Occitane en Provence** – A cosmetics and beauty brand offering a taste of life in Provence, South France. Offers products for the skin and body.
• **Le Temps** – A massage parlor with an approach which they call "ita-kimochi-ii" ("hurts so good!") that goes deep into the muscles to loosen them up and improve circulation.
• **Lush** – Fresh handmade cosmetics made from fruits, vegetables and plants.
• **Medi+Plus** – A drugstore selling everything such as supplements, household medicine, shampoo for traveling, and soap.
• **Steam Cream** – Skincare and cosmetics brand.
• **Stretchsalon Art Body** – Massage parlor specializing in improving the range of motion in the joints.
• **Taya Crystal World** – Beauty salon.
• **Temomin** – Massage services.
• **The Body Shop** – A full lineup of cosmetics made from natural materials.

Shops - Other Facilities & Services

• **Big Mama** – Clothes repair service, as well as pant leg hemming, skirt size adjusting, repairing knitted items, and repairing shoes, bags, and accessories.
• **Caricature Hosinoko** – Hand-drawn portraits.
• **Girls Mignon** – Photo booths that print stickers.
• **Ikspiari Card Service**

Counter – The reception area for the official IKSPIARI credit card, and related information.
• **JTB Desk** – Customer service desk for JTB travel agent customers; does not sell tours here.
• **Kokoni-Ta** – Fortune-telling services.
• **Maihama Mermaid**

Dental Clinic – Dental office with marine-themed interior.
• **Moreru Mignon** – Photo booths that prints stickers.
• **Studio Caraat** – Photo studio.
• **Tokyo Disney Resort Ticket Center** – Sells theme park tickets, TDR gift cards and annual passes.

Cinema Ikspiari

CINEMA IKSPIARI boasts of state-of-the-art theater equipment, digital sound that envelops the audience seats, and immersive widescreen. All the audience seats are stadium seats and are wide and comfortable for the ultimate movie-viewing experience.

The movie theater offers screenings of both Japanese language films and foreign films. With foreign movies, there is often the option of watched a dubbed version or the original language version with subtitles – this means there will likely be at least one or two movies playing in English with Japanese subtitles here when you visit.

See the schedule at ikspiari.com/cinema/schedule.html – this website is in Japanese only, so use Google Translate to help.

General admission tickets are ¥1,800, with discounts available for students, children, disabled people, and seniors upon presentation of ID. Special discounted screenings are available after 8:00 pm on the first day of the month, and every Wednesday for women.

Guests with Disabilities

This section covers procedures and accommodations Disney makes for guests visiting with disabilities. It includes people with mobility, hearing and visual impairments, and the Disability Access Service system for the theme parks. Tokyo Disney Resort calls its aim to include all guests in the fun 'barrier free'.

Mobility

Tokyo Disney Resort strives to allow all guests to utilize the main attraction entrances whenever possible, allowing the ride queuing system to be as fair as possible for all guests, whatever their physical or mental abilities.

However, accessibility does vary from attraction to attraction within the Disney Parks – disabled guests should ask a Cast Member at the entrance to an attraction for the appropriate entrance. Sometimes guests can ride in their ECVs; other times,

they must transfer to a wheelchair, and other times they must transfer to a ride vehicle.

To rent a wheelchair, or ECV/motorized scooter for the day, proceed to the stroller rental locations near the main entrance of each of the two theme parks. Guests may also bring their own into the parks.

If someone in your group with a disability needs to remain in a stroller in attraction queues at shows, visit Guest Relations at either theme park to receive

a "stroller as a wheelchair" tag to place on the stroller. You can also get these tags at all Disney hotels, from Ikspiari and each station on the Disney Resort Line.

Pricing is ¥500 per day for a wheelchair rental. Battery-assisted push wheelchairs are ¥1,000, and motorized wheelchairs (ECVs) are ¥2,000 for the day.

All Tokyo Disney Resort transportation accommodates both wheelchairs and ECVs.

Hearing

Guests with hearing disabilities have the following accommodations for them at the theme parks:

Attraction Story Papers - These introduce the story or narration used in selected attractions.

Sign Language Service - In Japanese only at select attractions, and when interacting with select Cast Members.

Visual

Guests with visual disabilities have the following accommodations for them at the theme parks: Braille guidebooks, stationary tactile maps, braille menus, and digital audio tours – all are available in Japanese only.

Also, scale models of the Disney characters and the attractions are available at Tokyo Disney Resort.

At Main Street House in Tokyo Disneyland or at Guest Relations in Tokyo DisneySea, guests may request to touch and handle

the models to get an idea of what the Disney characters look like, the shape of attraction seats, and special features of the attractions.

Guests may ask to handle the models at the attractions as well.

Disability Access Service (DAS)

The Disability Access Service (DAS) is designed for guests with disabilities (including non-apparent disabilities) that are not able to wait in a normal queue line – their privileges extend to their party.

The DAS system can be activated from Guest Relations at each theme park. Eligible guests are: holders of a physical disability certificate, mental disability certificate, or certificate for the cognitively challenged. Having a translation in Japanese is not required but may help.

At Guest Relations, the disabled guest will have their photo taken, and asked how many guests are in their party. This information is linked to the theme park ticket for the disabled guest.

How does the system work?

A disabled guest goes to an attraction, or character meet location (or another party member on behalf of the DAS guest) and asks the Cast Member there to use the DAS system – the ride attendant will issue the guest with a ride entry time (this will be roughly the same wait time as the current standby wait time). E.g., it is 2:00 pm and the wait time for an attraction is 45 minutes – the guest is given a 2:45 pm return time.

Until the ride entry time, the guest and their party will be able to wait in a separate area, along with their party, instead of in the queue until the designated time (you may not be able to experience the shows or presentations in the queue area). Guests will not be able to experience another attraction or Disney Character greeting while using this service. This service is not intended to shorten guests' wait time at an attraction or a Disney Character greeting location.

Depending on the degree of assistance needed or specific conditions at an attraction, DAS guests' wait time may be longer than that of the Guests standing in the standby line.

The system can be combined with Fastpass, and guests will still get the full FP entitlements, in addition to being able to use the system.

Separate Wait Service

Disney also offers a similar system to the Disability Access Service called the Separate Wait Service. Eligible guests are persons in wheelchairs, persons of advanced age, expectant mothers, and persons with disabilities. Guests do not need to register to use this service at Guest Relations.

To use this service, present the party's park tickets to the Cast Member at an attraction or a Disney Character greeting location. Guests who have difficulty standing in line for an extended period will be able to wait at a separate area instead of in the queue until the designated time (you may not be able to experience the shows or presentations in the queue area). All the other members of your party remain in the queue line. The guest using the Separate Wait Service will be able to rejoin your party at the boarding or greeting area.

Guests cannot experience another attraction or Disney Character greeting while using this service but can combine it with Fastpass. This service is not intended to shorten wait times at an attraction or a Disney Character greeting location.

More Information

If you require information regarding specific details of each aspect of your trip, Tokyo Disney Resort has created an incredibly detailed 66-page guide to the resort and all the attractions and facilities. You can download this at http://bit.ly/disabtdr.

Dining

There are many places to eat at the Tokyo Disney Resort. Food options vary from sandwich and snack locations to Counter Service (fast food) places, character buffets, Table Service dining, and even fine dining options. Eating can be as much a part of the experience as the attractions at the Tokyo Disney Resort.

Making Reservations

If you want to guarantee you will be able to dine at a specific restaurant, it is worth booking a table in advance. At the Tokyo Disney Resort, these reservations are called 'Priority Seating.'

You can make your restaurant reservation up to 30 days in advance, and if there is anywhere you would particularly like to eat, we recommend making reservations as soon as possible. Reservations can be made at https://reserve.tokyodisney resort.jp/en/, clicking

'Other' on the reservation box to the side, and then selecting 'Restaurants' from the dropdown box.

It is possible to make up to three dining reservations per day.

There are also extra reservation slots available on the day. These can be made from 9:00 am online via the above website, or from 10:00 am directly at the restaurant itself.

You do not need to be staying in a Disney hotel to

book a table at a restaurant. If you cannot attend a reservation, it is good practice to cancel it as soon as possible.

Unlike some other Disney resorts, there is not an option to pre-purchase dining plans or meal credits. Each restaurant is paid for on the day at the restaurant when dining.

Top Tip: If you wish to dine at Magellan's, specifically, it is worth booking as soon as reservations open - it is very popular.

Restaurant Types

Buffet – All-you-can-eat locations where you fill your plate from the food selection as many times as you want. Buffets may or may not include drinks.

Counter Service – Fast food. Look at the menus, pay for your food and collect it a few minutes later. You will find everything from burgers and chips to chicken, pizza, and pasta. Be aware that Disney 'fast'-food locations are notoriously slow, and a queue of just five or six people in front of you can easily mean a wait time of 20 to 30 minutes.

Buffeteria – Very similar to the Counter Service above. Except you do not pay first, then receive your goods. Instead, you pick up a tray, go through a set route like a cafeteria picking up what you want, and then pay at a register at the end. Similar to a school canteen/ cafeteria in layout.

Table Service – Where you order from a menu and are served by a waiter who brings food to your table.

Character Buffets – These are available all day and are all-you-can-eat places

where characters interact with you and take photos as you eat.

Top Tip: Whether it be a snack cart, a Counter Service location, or a Table Service restaurant, you usually do not have to order from a set menu. Ordering specific items 'a la carte' is completely fine, although it may save you money if you order certain set menu combinations.

In Japan, tipping is not a necessity and may be considered rude. There is no need to tip at any of the restaurants.

Good to Know

• For buffets, adult pricing applies for ages 13 and up, there are two separate pricing tiers for kids ages 4 to 6, and ages 7 to 12.
• Adults can order from the kids' menu at Counter Service and Buffeteria locations. At Table Service locations, this is not usually allowed.
• For an idea of how much food costs at the restaurants, see our parks chapters, which list set menu prices and a la carte main courses.
• Few restaurants offer a vegetarian option, and it is not customary to modify dishes or make substitutions in Japan. Please speak to a Cast Member who will do their best to help. It may be best to talk to Guest Relations about this as many of the Cast Members at the restaurants will likely not have the level of English to help with allergies or other dietary requirements. However, many restaurants do offer a "hypoallergenic menu," which Disney says "does not use the five major allergens (wheat, buckwheat, eggs, milk, peanuts) as raw materials."

Snacks

A huge part of Japanese Disney and theme park culture is snacks, especially snacks that look cute. You may well find that you can skip a meal and have a bunch of snacks instead.

Here are some of the most popular:

Tokyo Disneyland
• Bacon and egg rice ball – As the name says. Sold in Adventureland.
• Pizza Spring Roll – Mozarella, tomato sauce, and a giant spring roll all in one! Sold in Toontown.
• Mike Wazowski Melon Bread – A soft bun-like snack with a hint of melon flavor. You can find this throughout both parks, including the bakeries at the entrances of both parks.
• Mickey Waffles – This is a classic Disney staple, which can be found at the Great American Waffle Company and can be served with a variety of toppings.
• Mickey and Minnie Buns – These are two different snacks, each with its own flavor in the form of a steamed bun shaped like the classic Disney characters. Pick these up in World Bazaar.

Tokyo DisneySea
• Chandu Tail – Chicken bun shaped like the character Chandu's tail from the ride *'Sindbad's Storybook Voyage'*. Available at Sultan's Oasis.
• Donald Duck Flotation Ring – Shrimp bun, also known as Ukiwa Buns. Sold at Seaside Snacks.
• Gyoza Dog – Essentially a hot dog in a gyoza-style bun. Sold at Nautilus Galley.
• Green Alien Dumplings – These are three super-cute pounded rice balls shaped like the Green Aliens from Toy Story. Each has a different flavor – vanilla, strawberry, and chocolate. They are sold at both parks, including at the bakeries and in Tomorrowland (see photo).

Snacks are seasonal and change all the time. Pick up in-park leaflets for news on the latest additions.

Popcorn
Tokyo Disney Resort also

makes a huge deal out of its weird and wonderful popcorn flavors – they even include a whole panel on them on the park map. As well as the popcorn itself, you can buy cute popcorn holders in all kinds of design from Buzz Lightyear's box to Rapunzel's lantern.

Popcorn flavors include:
• Tokyo Disneyland – Soy Sauce and Butter, Barbecue, Caramel, Honey, Salt, Curry, Milk Chocolate, and Strawberry Milk
• Tokyo Disney Sea – Caramel, Honey, Garlic Shrimp, Salt, Strawberry, Curry, Milk Chocolate, and Chinese Chili

One portion of the popcorn is ¥400 for a regular box.

Tokyo Disney Resort for Walt Disney World Visitors

Many guests visit the Tokyo Disney Resort after having visited the Walt Disney World Resort in Florida. Both resorts immerse you in the Disney magic, but it is important to understand that the two locations are very different. This chapter helps you compare and contrast.

Local Customs

According to the latest available figures from the Oriental Land Company, 90.4% of visitors to Tokyo Disney Resort are Japanese, with only 9.6% coming from overseas – many of these will be from Korea and China. The number of Westerners in the parks is minimal on any given day. This compares to Walt Disney World's visitors from all corners of the world (but mainly Americans).

Many American customs do not apply to a Japanese audience and vice-versa. For example, the Japanese are incredibly orderly and like structure – they do not break the rules or try to have exceptions made. The customer service in Japan is also exemplary, and the Cast will go above and beyond to help – even more so than at Walt Disney World.

Tipping is also different. It is non-existent in Japan – and may even be considered offensive. In the US, it is a key part of the culture.

In general, guests are much more respectful at Japanese parks. There is no queue-jumping, or children on shoulders during parades, for example.

Lastly, the Japanese audience is a little bit more fashion-conscious than the crowds that visit Florida. Guests dress up to visit the theme parks in smart

clothing. Tank tops and shorts will be seen, but are a rarity, even in the hot weather.

The Japanese also love the concept of 'kawaii,' where everything must seem cute from food to clothes.

The Cast Members and Languages

The Cast Members in Florida and California, for the most part, go above and beyond, are incredibly polite, are never rude to a guest, have a passion for Disney, and do everything to make guests' stays as magical as possible.

However, the Cast Members at the Tokyo Disney Resort take this one step further and actively offer to help before you even ask. We have not ever seen a single Cast Member frown or look tired in Japan; it is simply not acceptable and seen as disrespectful to the guests.

In general, the Cast Members in the Japanese parks do not speak English or will only have a minimal grasp, so this is something to be aware of – they will help you find another Cast Member who can help, however.

It pays to learn some basic Japanese as well. It is basic manners to learn some of the language when visiting another country and at least say *Konichiwa* (hello) and *arigato gozaimasu* (thank you).

Resort Size and Transportation

The size difference between the two resorts is staggering: Walt Disney World is 47 square miles or 121 square kilometers. In comparison, Tokyo Disney Resort is just 2 square kilometers.

Even if you walked from one theme park to the other instead of using the Disney Resort Line, this is a 25-minute walk. Also, except for the Tokyo Disney Celebration Hotel, everything is on one central site.

However, at Walt Disney World, most journeys cannot be walked - not only because of the distance but because there are no sidewalks due to the sprawling size of Walt Disney World. Everything is a bus journey away from each other at Walt Disney World.

The advantage of Tokyo Disney Resort's small size is that you can walk throughout the whole resort, you can visit any of the other hotels easily, and you will spend less time traveling and more time enjoying yourself. The disadvantage is that there are fewer things to do: no water parks, fewer hotels, and crucially fewer theme parks (there are two in Tokyo, versus four in Florida).

Looking at the parks, Tokyo Disneyland Park is slightly

bigger than Magic Kingdom Park (114 acres vs. 107 acres). The two theme parks are very similar both in layout and in the attractions they offer.

Tokyo DisneySea doesn't have an equivalent at Walt Disney World – it spans 176 acres, making it slightly larger than Disney's Hollywood Studios (135 acres).

Annoyingly the two theme parks are placed back-to-back; unlike at Disneyland or Disneyland Paris, where you can walk from one park to the other in minutes, you will need to get the Disney Resort Line monorail or make the 25-minute walk between the two.

The resort hotels at Tokyo Disney Resort are also generally smaller than their Floridian counterparts.

If you have visited Disneyland Resort in

California, Tokyo Disney Resort is somewhere between Disneyland Resort and Walt Disney World, but size-wise is much more like Disneyland Resort.

The area where Tokyo Disney Resort is located is as much a significant transport hub as it is a world-class theme park resort. On TDR property, just minutes from the park entrances, you can hop on a subway that will whisk you to central Tokyo in only 15 minutes. You can also drive and be at non-Disney locations in just a few minutes too.

Tokyo Disney Resort is all very self-contained, so if you do fancy escaping the magic, it is easy to do - unlike in Florida! For some people, this freedom is a benefit, though others prefer the Floridian immersion of the Disney magic that lets them forget about the outside world.

Pricing

Disney trips can be very pricey when you take into account all of the costs. For this comparison, we are not including airfares or transportation costs to get to the resort. Generally speaking, the Tokyo Disney Resort is much cheaper than the American parks.

Hotels

At Tokyo Disney Resort, the cheapest room at a Value hotel (Tokyo Disney Celebration Hotel) starts at around ¥18,000 ($165) during low season per night. For a Deluxe hotel, you can pay ¥30,000 ($270) to ¥50,000 ($450) in the low season, depending on which hotel you choose.

For comparison, a comparable room at the Value-level Art of Animation in Florida starts from $180. A deluxe level room at the Contemporary resort begins at around $500 in the US or $700 for the Grand Floridian. The Floridian hotels are, therefore, pricier in general.

The difference is that in the US, you can frequently get significant discounts on these rooms; in Tokyo, the rooms sell out incredibly quickly, and they do not need to offer discounts. Realistically, the standard of the Japanese hotels is higher, and we would say the MiraCosta and Tokyo Disneyland Hotels are Disney's two best deluxe hotels in the world – and you cannot beat their location.

Park Tickets

A one-day entry ticket to Tokyo Disney Resort for one park is ¥7,500 ($69) for adults and ¥4,900 ($45) for children. At Walt Disney World, the equivalent ticket costs between $116 and $169 for adults and $111 to $164 for children depending on the date of the visit. For a one day visit, we can see that the price is 1.5x to 3.5x the cost in Florida.

Extending this to a 4-Day Ticket for comparison, at Tokyo, the price is $208 for an adult and $135 for a child. At Walt Disney World, a 4-Day ticket is $426 to $596 for an adult, and $408 to $578 for a child – these are for 1-park per day tickets at Disney World, as a park hopper adds on an extra $90 per person. Here we have an enormous difference in price once again where adult tickets are at least 2x-3x the price, and kids' tickets are 3x-4x the price.

Hands-down, the Tokyo Disney Resort, is more affordable for tickets. Although, of course, we should remember there are only two parks in Tokyo versus four in Orlando. More extended stays of 7 or 14-days in Florida become more affordable per day.

Food

Food prices at Tokyo Disney Resort are also significantly more affordable in Tokyo versus the American parks. Here are some examples:
• Bottled Drink (Soda) - $5 in Orlando, versus ¥360 ($3.30) at Tokyo
• Mickey Waffle - $5.80 in Orlando, versus ¥500 ($4.60) in Tokyo
• Popcorn - $4.50 in Orlando, versus ¥400 ($3.65) in Tokyo
• Counter Service meal (main and drink) - $17 in Orlando, versus ¥1,170 ($10.65) in Tokyo
• Table Service meal (starter, main, dessert) – $50 in Orlando (incl tip), versus ¥2,500 ($22) to ¥4,000 ($36) in Tokyo
• Buffet - $54 per adult and $29 per child (ages 3-9) at Walt Disney World versus ¥3,150 ($29) per adult and ¥2,000 ($18) for kids ages 7-12, and ¥1,250 ($11) for ages 4 to 6 in Tokyo.
• Signature Dining – $90 to $100 at Walt Disney World at California Grill or Citricos for dinner, versus ¥3,700 ($34) to ¥4,600 ($42) at lunch and ¥5,800 ($52) to ¥8,000 ($73) at dinner in Tokyo at Magellan's.

Remember, there is no tipping on the Table Service meals in Tokyo. Also, note that portions at Counter Service and Table Service meals are slightly smaller in Tokyo – but not enough to justify the vast price differences. At Walt Disney World, Table Service meals are generally a la carte, whereas, in Tokyo, guests typically choose from set menus.

Weather

Florida is known as the "sunshine state", and you can expect temperatures to reach 30°C (80-90°F) for much of the year. There are occasions where there are cold snaps and the temperature drops for a few days, but nothing to the levels seen in Tokyo.

Spring temperatures in Tokyo range from 6°C to 22°C (43°F to 72°F) during the day. There is a short rainy season in Spring, but apart from occasional showers, the weather is generally good.

Summer is comparable in both resorts where it can often be uncomfortably humid - June and July is Japan's rainy season. Summer temperatures in Tokyo range from 19°C to 32°C (66°F to 90°F) during the day, but the humidity means that the actual temperature feels much higher.

In the Fall/Autumn, frequent typhoons batter Tokyo with strong rain and wind. The days following a typhoon are incredibly calm and fine - perfect exploring weather. Autumn temperatures range from 9°C to 27°C (48°F to 81°F) during the day.

In Winter, snow in Tokyo is relatively rare, however, daytime temperatures range from 2°C to 12°C (35°F to 54°F).

Visitors to Walt Disney

World have to deal with Hurricane season from June to November when weather can get extreme, and hurricanes are possible.

Orlando visitors also deal with a tropical climate with daily thunderstorms in the summer, closing all outdoor attractions and drenching anyone not prepared. Tokyo's rain is more unpredictable, and is present year-round - thunderstorms are rarer.

Fastpass

Fastpass at Tokyo Disney Resort is a hybrid system where you can either book a Fastpass on the Tokyo Disney Resort app, or go to a Fastpass machine, insert your ticket and get a return time.

You are not able to select the time of this Fastpass and can only choose one Fastpass at a time (or every 2 hours – whichever is sooner) — Fastpass reservations are made on

the day itself, inside the theme park.

Walt Disney World has a fully digital Fastpass+ system. With Fastpass+ you can make ride reservations up to 60 days in advance on your smartphone or using in-park kiosks , or on the day itself.

Generally speaking, Fastpass reservations on the day run out much more quickly in Tokyo than in Orlando.

Unique Attractions and Details

Tokyo Disney Resort has many unique rides and shows which cannot be found at Walt Disney World.

Tokyo Disneyland is essentially a mash-up of Disneyland Park in California and Magic Kingdom Park in Florida. As such, it feels very familiar and doesn't have too many unique attractions.

In Tokyo Disneyland, in Adventureland, Western River Railroad is a unique land-only version of the railroad going around Magic Kingdom Park, and The Enchanted Tiki Room has a unique Stitch takeover in Tokyo.

In Critter Country, Beaver Brothers Explorer Canoes is unique.

In Fantasyland, Cinderella's Fairy Tale Hall is a fun walk through the castle. Pooh's Hunny Hunt is a unique ride and vastly superior to the Floridian Winnie-the-Pooh ride. The Enchanted Tale of Beauty and the Beast attraction will also be unique when it opens in April 2020 – this looks incredibly fun.

Toontown is unique with all its rides, although it is very similar to the one in Disneyland, Anaheim.

Finally, in Tomorrowland Stitch Encounter is similar to Turtle Talk with Crush, but with Stitch (Japanese only). Monsters, Inc. Ride & Go Seek! is a completely original dark ride, which is

great fun.

Tokyo DisneySea has many more unique attractions. As you enter the park into the Mediterranean Harbor, you will encounter the Venetian Gondolas, which is unlike any other Disney park attraction anywhere. Fortress Explorations and the Leonardo Challenge are unique interactive experiences. The DisneySea Transit Steamer Line is an immersive transportation option that cannot be compared with anything at Walt Disney World.

Tower of Terror! has an entirely different story, interior, and drop profile to that in the states, meaning that it is its own unique experience. S.S. Columbia is not present in any other Disney park, and DisneySea Electric Railway gives you a unique perspective on the park.

In Port Discovery, Aquatopia is a fun, unique experience; Nemo & Friends Searider is also wholly original.

Over in Lost River Delta, Indiana Jones Adventure is an almost exact clone of the attraction at Disneyland, but there is no equivalent in Florida. The Raging Spirits roller coaster is unique, too, although it is essentially the same ride as the Indiana Jones rollercoaster in Paris.

Mermaid Lagoon is a unique, mostly-indoor kids area; all seven attractions here are unique, including the show with Ariel.

Arabian Coast has a unique double-decker carousel, a unique 3D show at the Magic Lamp Theater, and the cute and unmissable boat ride in Sindbad's Storybook Voyage.

Finally, Mysterious Island contains two unique attractions (as well as an erupting volcano!) with the immersive 20,000 Leagues Under the Sea and the fast-paced Journey to the Center of the Earth.

The parks also have unique parades, shows, themed areas, and night-time spectaculars.

2020 Seasonal Events

Tokyo Disney Resort offers its guests something different throughout the year, with seasonal and special events that celebrate traditions such as Easter, Halloween, and Christmas, as well as Disney-themed seasons. Each seasonal event will bring new decorations, entertainment, food, and merchandise. These are all included in your regular park ticket unless otherwise stated.

Very Very Minnie! at Tokyo Disneyland

10th January to 19th March 2020

A new show and parade will be performed at the park daily in anticipation of the new Minnie's Style Studio, which opens in April 2020.

The 25-minute show, entitled 'It's Very Minnie', will be played at Showbase replacing 'One Man's Dream II.' In the show, Minnie Mouse is joined by her Disney Friends in this musical revue. Music and costumes from Park entertainment over the years are brought back in scenes of various styles themed to Latin music, romance, and club dancing.

The parade, entitled 'Very Minnie Remix,' stops in six different places along the parade route for a special performance of music and dancing from past shows. The parade will be presented in three versions, each focusing on different shows depending on the day and where the parade stops. Accordingly, Guests will be able to enjoy a different performance every time they view the parade.

Pixar Playtime at Tokyo DisneySea

10th January to 19th March 2020

Tokyo DisneySea will again offer the special event, "Pixar Playtime," which gives guests a variety of experiences themed to the world of Disney and Pixar films.

The Pixar Characters gather at Mediterranean Harbor for "Pixar Playtime Pals." Guests of all ages will be able to enjoy their favorite Pixar Characters in this participatory stage show, featuring for the first time this year Bo Peep from Toy Story 4.

Other entertainment programs include "Lightning McQueen Victory Lap" themed to the Cars film series, "Chef Remy & You," featuring Remy from the film Ratatouille, and more.

Duffy's Heartwarming Days

10th January to 19th March 2020

This program at Tokyo DisneySea reflects the warm and gentle world of Duffy and his friends. Special decorations around the Cape Cod area, merchandise, and menu items will feature designs of the friends happily making waffles. You can also meet Duffy himself next to Cape Cod Cook-Off, while ShellieMay will be at the Village Greeting Place. Duffy and ShellieMay will be dressed in new costumes themed to waffle-making.

Disney Easter at Tokyo DisneySea

22nd March to 12th June 2020

This event will include props and decorations around the theme parks, a seasonal show and other seasonal entertainment, as well as special food and merchandise. Disney has not yet revealed specific details for 2020 but you can expect Easter eggs and bunnies abound as per previous years.

Happy Fair with Baymax at Tokyo Disneyland

4th June to 1st November 2020

Celebrate the opening of the new Baymax attraction in Tomorrowland with this program, which features decorations, photo locations, merchandise and menu items themed to the Disney film Big Hero 6.

Duffy and Friend's Sunny Fun

4th June to 26th August 2020

Guests will enjoy the world of Duffy and Friends in this program that offers merchandise, menu items at Tokyo DisneySea, and decorations inspired by Duffy and Friends enjoying a bright summer day at the beach in Cape Cod.

Disney Pirates Summer at Tokyo DisneySea

1st July to 2nd September 2020

This popular event from previous years returns to Tokyo DisneySea and brings the world of the Disney Pirates of the Caribbean film series to Tokyo DisneySea. At Mediterranean Harbor, guests can enjoy a show featuring Captain Jack Sparrow, Captain Barbossa and their motley crew of pirates; this show features a lot of water, so be prepared to get very wet as cannons of water are fired right at the audience!

Disney Halloween (Both Parks)

11th September to 1st November 2020

Each Park will offer its own unique "Disney Halloween" event.

At Tokyo Disneyland, ghosts will welcome Guests to their spooky, ghostly version of the park with the Spooky Boo Parade. You can also expect Haunted Mansion to have a *Nightmare Before Christmas* makeover.

Tokyo DisneySea will feature sea witches who have devised a plan to bring the Halloween festivities under their control. The Festival of

Mystique harbor show at Porto Paradiso will return as an eerie air of foreboding hangs over the festivities.

Guests will also be able to dress up as Disney characters while visiting during this season – guests do make an amazing effort with their costumes, and this really adds to the season.

Disney Christmas (Both Parks)

10th November to 25th December 2020

At Tokyo Disneyland, Guests will enjoy themed pop-up storybooks full of Christmas fun with Disney friends.

A Christmas parade, decorations, merchandise, and menu items will help bring to life pages from storybooks showing the Disney characters having fun at Christmastime. The Tokyo Disneyland Electrical Parade Dreamlights even takes on a magical Christmas twist!

Tokyo DisneySea will feature an entertaining, colorful revue presented at Mediterranean Harbor. Guests will be enchanted with the live performances that create a wonderful holiday mood unique to Tokyo DisneySea.

You can also expect Haunted Mansion to have a Nightmare Before Christmas makeover until the start of January. The Country Bear Jamboree Jingle Bell Jamboree also appears for the Christmas season (Japanese only).

New Year Season (Both Parks)

1st to 5th January 2021

Celebrate the ringing in of the new year at Tokyo Disney Resort.

Special decorations go up for this event on 26th December each year and are removed on 6th January. Unique entertainment is also provided in the form of a short parade at Tokyo Disneyland and a quick show at Tokyo DisneySea – this will be performed a few times daily throughout the season. Mickey Mouse and his friends will be dressed in kimonos to welcome Guests in Japanese style.

New Year's Eve Special Event (Both Parks)

31st December 2020

This is an extra ticketed event on 31st December each year. Both theme parks close to regular guests at around 5:00 pm or 6:00 pm. Then from 8:00 pm, only guests with event tickets can enter the two theme parks for the special New Year's Eve event.

The parks then remain open for 26 hours straight until 10:00 pm on 1st January. From 4:00 am on 1st January, you are also able to park-hop.

The parks' regular attractions, shows, and other entertainment will be available during the New Year Event, and at midnight a 10-minute firework show will ring in the new year. Tickets for this unique 26-hour event cost around ¥10,000 per person.

Tickets are difficult to get for the New Year's Eve Event – you can either enter an online lottery on the TDR website from September or book a Disney hotel and get the ticket at the hotel itself. Finally, you can also book an Official hotel (such as the Hilton Tokyo Bay) and buy a ticket at the hotel itself. Hotel rooms sell out very quickly for this date, and you may need to call to make reservations over the New Year instead of doing it online.

The Future

Tokyo Disney Resort is always working on something new an exciting. Take a peek into the future of the resort here!

New Toy Story Hotel (2021)

A new family-friendly Disney hotel based on the Disney·Pixar "Toy Story" films is coming soon to Tokyo Disney Resort!

From the hotel exterior to the spacious gardens, guests will enjoy a world where everything looks like it is made of toys. The guest rooms are inspired by

Andy's bedroom. The hotel will hold about 600 rooms, and also include dining and shopping. We think this will be a 'Value'-style hotel like *Tokyo Disney Celebration Hotel* or slightly higher; it will not be a Deluxe hotel like the Hotel MiraCosta, Disneyland Hotel or Ambassador Hotel.

The hotel will be located on the main Tokyo Disney Resort land opposite Bayside Station.

We expect the hotel to have access to Happy15 early entry as with the other Disney hotels.

DisneySea "Fantasy Springs" (2022)
10th January to 19th March 2020

Tokyo DisneySea will become even more amazing in 2022 with an eighth Port of Call starring the Disney films Frozen, Tangled, and Peter Pan. This newest port will be themed to magical springs that lead to a world of Disney fantasy and will include four new attractions.

Guests will discover Arendelle after the events in "Frozen," once the kingdom has opened its gates to visitors. A heartwarming new attraction will take guests by boat to experience the story of Elsa and Anna while enjoying iconic songs from the hit film, and a new restaurant will be located inside Arendelle Castle.

Another new area will invite guests into the charming forest where Rapunzel's tower awaits. Guests can board gondolas for a

romantic tour of Rapunzel's "best day ever" as she journeys with Flynn to the lantern festival for an unforgettable finale. Also on the menu is a restaurant inspired by the hideout of the humorous band of thugs in the movie.

Neverland will come to life for guests, including Captain Hook's pirate ship and Skull Rock. The area will feature two new attractions and a restaurant inspired by the Lost Boys hideout. In the first attraction, guests will fly over the jungles of

Neverland with Peter Pan to rescue Wendy's younger brother, John, in a battle with Captain Hook. The second attraction will immerse guests in the world of Pixie Hollow where Tinker Bell and her fairy friends live.

A new deluxe resort hotel will also open inside Tokyo DisneySea as part of the Fantasy Springs expansion plan. The hotel will feature 475 deluxe and luxury guest rooms, two restaurants and a merchandise shop.

Tokyo Disneyland Map

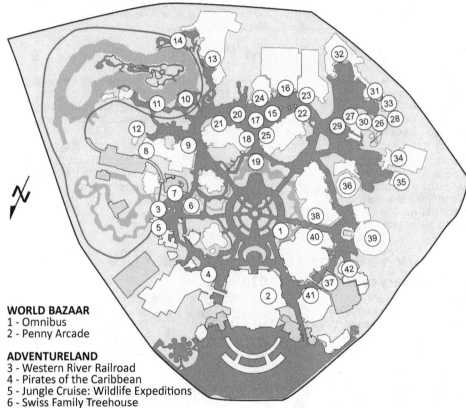

WORLD BAZAAR
1 - Omnibus
2 - Penny Arcade

ADVENTURELAND
3 - Western River Railroad
4 - Pirates of the Caribbean
5 - Jungle Cruise: Wildlife Expeditions
6 - Swiss Family Treehouse
7 - The Enchanted Tiki Room: Stitch Presents "Aloha E Komo Mai!"

WESTERNLAND
8 - Westernland Shootin' Gallery
9 - Country Bear Theater
10 - Mark Twain Riverboat
11 - Tom Sawyer Island Rafts

CRITTER COUNTRY
12 - Big Thunder Mountain
13 - Splash Mountain
14 - Beaver Brothers Explorer Canoes

FANTASYLAND
15 - Alice's Tea Party
16 - "it's a small world"
17 - Castle Carrousel
18 - Snow White's Adventures
19 - Cinderella's Fairy Tale Hall
20 - Dumbo The Flying Elephant
21 - Peter Pan's Flight
22 - Pinocchio's Daring Journey
23 - Pooh's Hunny Hunt
24 - Haunted Mansion
25 - Mickey's Philharmagic
34 - Enchanted Tale of Beauty and the Beast
35 - Fantasyland Forest Theater

TOONTOWN
26 - Gadget's Go Coaster
27 - Goofy's Paint 'n' Play House
28 - Chip 'n Dale's Treehouse
29 - Minnie's Style Studio
30 - Donald's Boat
31 - Minnie's House
32 - Roger Rabbit's Car Toon Spin
33 - Mickey's House and Meet Mickey

TOMORROWLAND
36 - The Happy Ride with Baymax
37 - Star Tours: The Adventures Continue
38 - Stitch Encounter
39 - Space Mountain
40 - Buzz Lightyear's Astro Blasters
41 - Monsters, Inc., Ride & Go Seek!
42 - Showbase

Tokyo DisneySea Map

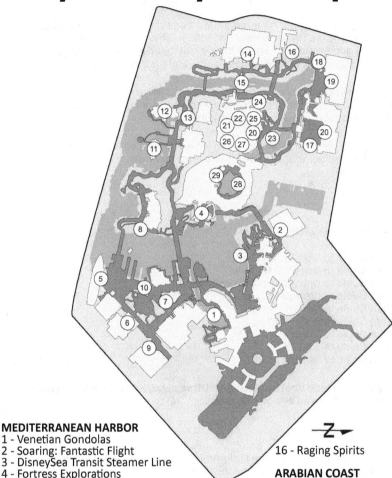

MEDITERRANEAN HARBOR
1 - Venetian Gondolas
2 - Soaring: Fantastic Flight
3 - DisneySea Transit Steamer Line
4 - Fortress Explorations

AMERICAN WATERFRONT
5 - Turtle Talk
6 - Tower of Terror
7 - DisneySea Electric Railway
8 - DisneySea Transit Steamer Line
9 - Toy Story Mania!
10 - Big City Vehicles

PORT DISCOVERY
11 - Aquatopia
12 - DisneySea Electric Railway
13 - Nemo & Friends SeaRider

LOST RIVER DELTA
14 - Indiana Jones Adventure: Temple of the Crystal Skull
15 - DisneySea Transit Steamer Line

16 - Raging Spirits

ARABIAN COAST
17 - Caravan Carousel
18 - Jasmine's Flying Carpets
19 - Sindbad's Storybook Voyage
20 - The Magic Lamp Theater

MERMAID LAGOON
21 - Ariel's Playground
22 - Jumpin' Jellyfish
23 - Scuttle's Scooters
24 - Flounder's Flying Fish Coaster
25 - Blowfish Balloon Race
26 - Memaid Lagoon Theater
27 - The Whirlpool

MYSTERIOUS ISLAND
28 - 20,000 Leagues Under the Sea
29 - Journey to the Center of the Earth

A Special Thanks

Thank you very much for reading our travel guide. We hope this book has made a big difference to your trip to Tokyo Disney Resort, and that you have found some tips that will save you time, money and hassle! Remember to take this guide with you when you are visiting the resort. This guide is available in both digital and printed formats.

If you have any feedback about any element of the guide, or have noticed changes in the parks that differ from what is in the book, do let us know by sending us a message. To contact us, visit our website at www.independentguidebooks.com.

If you enjoyed the guide, we would love for you to leave a review on Amazon or wherever you have purchased this guide. Your reviews make a huge difference in helping other people find this guide. Thank you.

Have a magical time!

If you have enjoyed this guide, other travel guides in this series include:

• The Independent Guide to Walt Disney World
• The Independent Guide to Universal Orlando
• The Independent Guide to Universal Studios Hollywood
• The Independent Guide to Disneyland
• The Independent Guide to Disneyland Paris
• The Independent Guide to Hong Kong
• The Independent Guide to Tokyo
• The Independent Guide to London
• The Independent Guide to New York City

Coming soon in 2020 are guide books to Shanghai Disneyland, Hong Kong Disneyland and Universal Studios Japan. Keep an eye out for these.

Photo credits:

The following photos have been used from Flickr (unless otherwise stated) in this guide under a Creative Commons license. Thank you to: Ambassador Hotel – alberth2; Celebration Hotel – tokyodisneyresort.jp; Swiss Family Treehouse – ume-y; Big Thunder Mountain – Ruth and Dave; Snow White's Adventures – Loren Javier; Pinnochio's Daring Journey – Harshlight; Pirates - 'gwaar'; Treehouse - 'ume-y'; Splash - Evelyn Lim;

Other images are from Unsplash contributors.

Some images and descriptions are copyright The Walt Disney Company, Tokyo Disney Resort, and The Oriental Land Company, and are used under Fair Use. No copyright infringement is intended.

CPSIA information can be obtained
at www.ICGtesting.com
Printed in the USA
BVHW010213290620
582533BV00005B/299

9 781838 047825